D0443840

BY DANIEL COHEN

THE MILLBROOK PRESS
BROOKFIELD, CONNECTICUT

Library of Congress Cataloging-in-Publication Data
Cohen, Daniel, 1936–
Cults / by Daniel Cohen.
p.   cm.
Includes bibliographical references and index.

Summary: An accurate and rational discussion of
cults including the subjects of satanism, witches,
mind control, and attempts at deprogramming.

ISBN 1-56294-324-3 (lib. bdg.)
1. Cults—United States—Juvenile literature.   2. United States—
Religion—1960– Juvenile literature.   [1. Cults.]   I. Title.
BL2525.C626   1994
291.9′0973—dc20   94-966   CIP   AC

Photos courtesy of AP/Wide World Photos: pp. 9, 18, 27,
47, 55, 104, 114; UPI/Bettmann: p. 24; Author's collection:
pp. 35, 40, 60, 64, 66, 69, 92, 96, 109; David Wilson: p. 120.

Published by The Millbrook Press
2 Old New Milford Road, Brookfield, Connecticut 06804

Contents

CULTS

WACO AND JONESTOWN

The events that led to the terrible and terrifying end of the Branch Davidian cult in Waco, Texas, were played out before a live television audience for a period of fifty-one days early in 1993.

The Branch Davidian cult, a tiny offshoot of the Seventh-Day Adventists, had been in existence for some twenty years. In the late 1980s, the old Davidian leadership had been challenged by an energetic and charismatic young convert named Vernon Howell. The conflict resulted in an armed confrontation from which Howell emerged the victor. However, he was also arrested and tried on a variety of charges, including possession of illegal weapons. He was acquitted, and his weapons were returned to him.

By this time Howell had changed his name to David Koresh—for David, the biblical king, and Koresh, the Hebrew name for the Persian king Cyrus the Great. Cyrus had helped the ancient Hebrews return to power in their homeland, and is spoken of approvingly in the Bible.

The new leader of the Branch Davidians was a poorly educated young man who had once aspired to be a rock musician. He possessed a phenomenal memory for Scripture, which he could recite and interpret for hours on end. While his theology made no sense at all to most people who heard him, some found his rambling sermons compelling. Koresh made several trips to other countries—England, Australia, and Israel among them—in search of converts. He picked up a few, but only a few. David Koresh's Branch Davidians never had more than about 150 deeply committed followers. Most, however, were quite well educated, and those who believed in him believed with all their heart and soul. They abandoned themselves to a harsh life of difficult physical labor, spartan living conditions, and physical isolation. They submitted to Koresh's bizarre and often brutal treatment.

Not everyone who had a brush with the Branch Davidians remained under Koresh's spell. There were plenty of dropouts who gave gruesome accounts of sexual abuse and arms stockpiling within the cult. They told of Koresh's growing obsession with the apocalypse—the fast-approaching time in which the world as we know it would be destroyed—and the belief that only those who followed the teachings of David Koresh would be saved.

ATHOUGH HIS FOLLOWERS WERE FEW IN NUMBER, DAVID KORESH'S NAME BECAME A HOUSEHOLD WORD IN 1993 BY WAY OF HIS ILL-FATED STANDOFF WITH FEDERAL OFFICIALS.

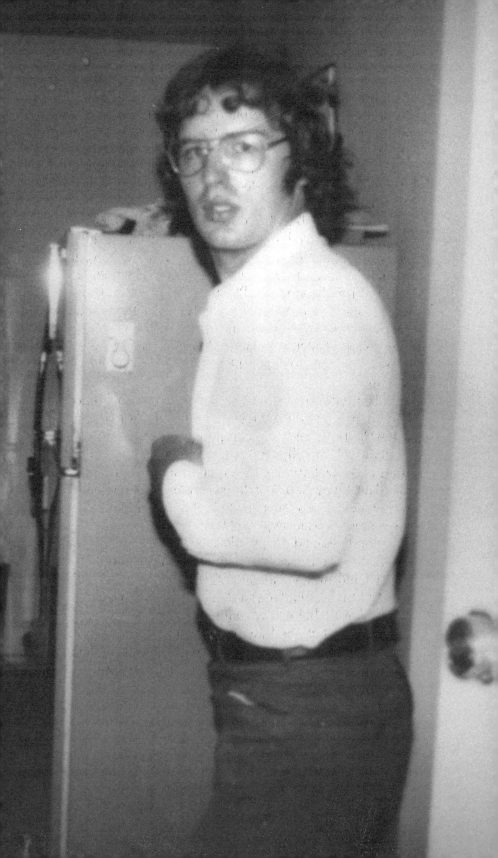

The group purchased a ranch outside of Waco, Texas, and proceeded to build a fortified compound so that they could protect themselves from a hostile outside world and presumably from some of the violence of the apocalypse, which they believed to be imminent. The media referred to the place as Ranch Apocalypse.

The Branch Davidians had become well known to both state and federal law enforcement authorities because of their weapons stockpiling and the charges leveled by former cult members and the families of some current members. The Bureau of Alcohol, Tobacco and Firearms (ATF), the federal agency that regulates the sale of weapons, decided that the Davidians were breaking the law and on February 28, 1993, staged a raid on the compound in order to arrest David Koresh.

The raid was a disaster. Somehow the Davidians had been tipped off to the plan. As the well-armed ATF agents approached the compound, they were confronted with equally well-armed cult members. Both sides may have miscalculated, and there was a shootout. Four agents and an unknown number of Davidians were killed. The agents backed off and called in reinforcements, and a siege began.

For fifty-one days, people across the United States were treated to live televised updates of the standoff on the evening news. The Branch Davidians, who had been virtually unknown, suddenly were famous. Every scrap of available evidence about Koresh and his followers was unearthed and displayed on television or printed in the newspapers. In the early months of 1993 the standoff at Waco became a national obsession.

The drama seemed to ebb and flow. There were reports that Koresh was waiting for a particular date to pass before surrendering. Some of the cult members—including many, though by no means all, of the children—left the compound, and there were hopes of a peaceful ending.

The authorities were by turns conciliatory, allowing Koresh to broadcast one of his rambling religious messages on the radio, and frustrated by what they saw as a series of evasions and lies on the part of the cult leader. Authorities tried to break the spirit of those holding out in the compound by playing recorded Buddhist chants and other unusual things through loudspeakers near the buildings. The technique didn't work and was abandoned when the public began to ridicule such tactics.

More seriously, authorities began to fear for the lives of those still in the compound. Koresh might order his followers to commit suicide rather than surrender, or he could provoke a shoot-out with the authorities. There was also concern about an outbreak of disease because the isolated compound lacked adequate sanitation.

Advice, solicited and unsolicited, came in from a huge number of cult "experts." It ranged from ordering an immediate commando-style raid on the compound to simply letting the people inside go. Koresh was described as everything from a homicidal, child-molesting lunatic to a sincere, if somewhat misguided, Christian leader.

Finally, on April 19, the authorities decided that they had waited long enough. Early that morning, officials sent an armored tank loaded with nonlethal tear gas rumbling toward Ranch Apocalypse's main building. Those inside the compound were given a few minutes' warning, in hope that the threat would bring them out. If that failed, then the tear gas should do the job. Many of the Davidians had gas masks, but the adult-sized masks would not have fitted the children properly. The compound, however was quite large, and there were areas that could not be reached by the gas. There was some confusion at first, but the hoped-for mass exodus did not take place.

The progress of the assault on the cult compound was being closely monitored back in Washington by government officials, right up to the president. Everyone realized that something very important was happening. No one knew what the end would be, but no one expected what finally happened.

There were repeated assaults by the tank. Shortly after noon, flames were spotted in the compound. Within a very few minutes the entire complex of buildings, which were made of wood and built without any thought of fire prevention, was engulfed. A dry wind blowing at 30 miles (48 kilometers) per hour whipped the flames. A few individuals were able to escape the conflagration. One woman, her clothes afire, ran from the building, but suddenly stopped and tried to run back in. Federal Bureau of Investigation (FBI) agents on the scene were able to catch her and put out the flames.

In less than half an hour it was all over. The Branch Davidian compound had burned to the ground. There was only a handful of survivors. Seventy-nine Davidians, many of them young children, had perished along with their leader, David Koresh. The aim of the siege and the assault had been to save lives—this was the worst possible result. Ranch Apocalypse had lived up to its grim name.

As with the initial raid on the compound in February, the exact sequence of events is unclear. The FBI reported that its agents had seen cult members actually starting the fire. One of those who had been negotiating with the Davidians shouted, "They've torched the compound." Survivors, however, insist that the fire had not been deliberately set by cult members but had started as a direct result of the tear gas assault.

Controversy also swirls about the question of how the cult members died. Most of the bodies were badly burned, but evidence showed that some, including David Koresh himself, had been shot. Did they commit suicide, or were some shot by more fanatical members while trying to escape?

There have been investigations, reports, and trials. But probably no explanation will satisfy everyone. Emotions run too deep. The tactics of the siege and the final assault will be debated endlessly among law enforcement officials, psychologists, and even the clergy.

For most ordinary people who watched the tragedy unfold during the early months of 1993, exact explanations are relatively unimportant. What sticks in most people's minds is the gruesome spectacle of a group so devoted to a leader and a philosophy—one that most consider strange and even insane—that they were willing to die rather than surrender.

Yet no one should really have been surprised. This sort of thing has happened many, many times throughout history. One of the most horrifying cases ever, one that puts even the spectacle of the destruction of the Branch Davidians into the shade, happened only fifteen years earlier.

On November 18, 1978, a charismatic preacher named Jim Jones led more than 900 of his followers in a mass suicide ritual that he called the "White Night." Most people call it the Jonestown Tragedy or, more appropriately, the Jonestown Horror.

There was nothing in the appearance or early career of the handsome, dark-haired Jones to suggest a wild-eyed fanatic or homicidal madman. As a boy growing up in Lynn, Indiana, he had shown a passion for religion and a talent for public speaking. He preached to local congregations and was appointed a student pastor in the Methodist church.

Jim Jones, however, was not to be confined by an established denomination. By 1956, he had broken away from the Methodists and founded his own church, called Community Unity, in Indianapolis. His church ultimately came to be known as the Peoples Temple.

Jones developed a doctrine that mixed basic Christian evangelism and socialism. He envisioned a world in which people would live together without racial divisions, economic inequality, or private property. His sermons were full of hope for the creation of an earthly paradise.

Side by side with the hope there appeared a strong undercurrent of fear and paranoia. Jones began to talk vaguely of "forces" that were out to destroy his church. He also became increasingly obsessed with the belief that the world was about to be destroyed in a cataclysmic nuclear war. At the time, fear of nuclear war was both widespread and justified. Few, however, reacted as strongly as did the Reverend Jones. He had read an article about how certain parts of the world might survive the effects of nuclear war. South America was said to be relatively safe. So he moved his family to Belo Horizonte, Brazil. The place did not live up to his expectations, and he was soon back preaching in Indianapolis. Still not satisfied, Jones began looking around for a new safe haven, and he found one in Redwood City, California, north of San Francisco.

In California, Jones's religious/political message found a large and sympathetic audience. There were soon branches of the Peoples Temple in San Francisco and Los Angeles. At its height the Peoples Temple had thousands of followers. Attracted by the white preacher's message of racial harmony, most of those in Jones's flock were black. They were also mostly poor, yet they contributed large portions of their meager incomes to Jim Jones, making him both wealthy and powerful.

Jones was no simple religious racketeer, yet there was much of the conscious charlatan about him. He often staged phony healing ceremonies in which some of his followers portrayed sick people who were dramatically "cured" when Jones laid his hands upon them. Jones seemed to justify the charade by saying that people needed miracles to believe in.

What this fraud really showed was Jim Jones's growing contempt for his followers. He began demanding increasing control over their lives, threatening and humiliating all who failed to obey his orders with unquestioning loyalty.

Yet the public perception of Jim Jones was very different. Here was a man who both preached and practiced racial equality. Volunteers from the Peoples Temple staffed an array of socially worthwhile projects from soup kitchens to day-care centers. Jones ingratiated himself with California politicians by both his charm and his ability to solidly deliver a bloc of thousands of voters. He was appointed chairman of the San Francisco Housing Authority. He had a well-publicized meeting with Rosalynn Carter, wife of President Jimmy Carter.

Eventually, it became impossible for a group as large as the Peoples Temple to operate in unexamined secrecy in a place like California. Former Temple members began talking to the press about Jones's increasingly unstable behavior. News organizations began taking a hard look at Jim Jones and his flock. It was only a matter of time until the underside of the Peoples Temple would be in the full glare of publicity. Jones might have found himself the target of criminal investigation for the improper use of funds.

Jones had anticipated the problems. He had spoken publicly about his desire to form a commune somewhere far from the evils of contemporary American society. He had already leased several thousand acres in the coastal jungles of the small South American country of Guyana. In the late summer of 1977, Jones and hundreds of his followers abruptly departed for Guyana, to a place that he had named Jonestown.

The weak and indulgent government of Guyana exercised virtually no control over the remote settlement. Jones sent back fund-raising brochures describing the idyllic existence at the paradise in the jungle. Reality was horrifyingly different. In his isolated kingdom, Jim Jones and a handful of aides exercised total control over the residents of Jonestown.

They were forced to work up to twelve hours a day in heat that regularly topped 100 degrees Fahrenheit

(38 degrees Celsius). At night they had to attend services where Jones preached for hours. Any infraction of the commune's erratic rules, any show of defiance, was punished by public flogging. Children were not exempt. Jones routinely humiliated even his most obedient and docile followers.

Yet the paranoid Jones still could not feel secure. He continually harangued cult members about "enemies" from the outside. Rather than being overwhelmed, Jones said, it would be better to commit "revolutionary suicide." He held rehearsals for a mass suicide that he called the "White Night."

The "enemies" finally arrived on November 17, 1978. A delegation led by Congressman Leo Ryan of California came to Jonestown in two small planes. A number of Congressman Ryan's constituents were worried about relatives in Jonestown. Jones greeted the delegation with apparent friendliness and showed them around the commune. During the visit a few members passed a note to Congressman Ryan indicating that they wished to return to the United States with him. This appeared to upset Jones, but he agreed to let them go if they wished.

All seemed perfectly normal as the congressman and his party drove to the jungle airstrip for their return flight. Then, suddenly and without warning, several of Jones's followers began shooting at them with automatic weapons. Congressman Ryan and four others were killed at once. Other members of the delegation fled into the jungle to escape the assassins. A few managed to board one of the planes and flee. They had in their possession films of the shooting.

The killing of a U.S. congressman, documented by the dramatic films, made this a major news story—but

ONE OF THE MORE GROTESQUE OUTCOMES OF CULTISM
CARRIED TO AN EXTREME WAS THE MASS SUICIDE-MURDER
OF JIM JONES'S FOLLOWERS IN JONESTOWN, GUYANA.

it was only the beginning. After the shooting nothing was heard from Jonestown. It took Guyanese troops a full day to reach the remote area.

The first stories that filtered out were of finding a hundred or more bodies. As the hours went on the total went up, as bodies were found piled upon bodies. The final total was 914 dead—practically everyone in Jonestown, including Jim Jones himself.

After the shooting, Jones had gathered his followers for the White Night ritual—this time for real. A large vat had been filled with a flavored drink mixed with poison. Jones's most loyal followers acted as armed guards and prodded those who held back. But most drank the poisoned mixture willingly. Parents gave doses to their children. Jones himself died from a gunshot wound to the head; whether he shot himself or ordered an aide to shoot him is unknown.

A handful of people managed to escape the deadly ritual by hiding in the jungle. A tape recorder that had been left running recorded the madman's final sermon.

Though virtually every detail of the Jonestown Horror is now well known, at its core Jonestown, like Waco, remains a terrifying mystery. How could so many people be led to their death by one man's insanity? What is the power that cults and their leaders can exercise over their followers?

WHAT IS
A CULT?

Practically everyone would agree that David Koresh's Branch Davidians and Jim Jones's Peoples Temple were cults. But trying to decide what is and what is not a cult is not as easy as these extreme examples would make it seem.

The dictionaries are not much help. The authoritative *Oxford English Dictionary* notes that in its original form, the word *cult* simply meant "a particular form of worship or devotion."

The *Random House Dictionary* defines a cult as: "a group or sect bound together by devotion to or veneration of the same thing, person, ideal, etc." and "a religion that is considered or held to be false or unorthodox." The Chicago columnist Sydney Harris once wrote: "My religion is a denomination, yours is a sect, his is a cult."

In many ways the history of America was shaped by the actions of groups that could legitimately be defined as cults. The people who called themselves the Pilgrims, who came from Europe aboard the *Mayflower* and landed in Plymouth, Massachusetts, in the fall of 1620, were a small, radical religious group better known as the Separatists. In the eyes of their contemporaries these Separatists were religious fanatics who fled their homeland to the wilderness so that they could practice their own peculiar brand of religion away from the temptations of civilization.

Then there were the Quakers, whose doctrines and way of life seemed even odder to the conventionally religious folk of England than the beliefs and ways of the Separatists. In the New World, the Quakers were persecuted more severely by the descendants of the Pilgrims than they had been by the established Church of England. Though they had fled religious persecution, the Pilgrims were so convinced of the truth of their own doctrines that they refused to tolerate anyone who did not believe as they did.

There were many other small, religiously unorthodox immigrant groups—the Shakers, the Amish, the Hutterites, the Inspirationists, the Moravians, the Harmony Society, to name just a few—who came to America in order to practice their own particular form of worship.

The wide open spaces of America were not only a magnet for cults, they were also a fertile breeding ground for them.

Perhaps no group better illustrates the difficulties of determining what a cult is than the Church of Jesus Christ of Latter-day Saints, better known as the Mormon Church. Today the Mormon Church is a large, well-established, highly conservative, and very respectable religious group. There was, however, nothing conservative or respectable about its origins.

The founder of the Mormon Church was an unsuccessful young farmer and sometime treasure hunter named Joseph Smith, of Palmyra, New York. Palmyra is located in that part of upstate New York that was once known as "the Burnt-Over District." The name was given to the area because it was regularly swept by the fires of religious enthusiasm. Smith himself had once been found guilty of being "a disorderly person and an impostor."

In 1827, Joseph Smith claimed that at some earlier date he had found some golden plates inscribed in a language he called "reformed Egyptian." There is no reliable record that anyone else ever saw these golden plates. When translated by Smith they gave a mythic history of America's pre-Columbian inhabitants, in a language that resembles the King James translation of the Bible. No non-Mormon scholar has ever found a scrap of evidence to support the account. However, it became the Book of Mormon, named after the ancient American who allegedly had written it. The Book of Mormon was followed by a flow of revelations from Smith.

A small number of people who regarded him as a "seer" and a prophet gathered around Joseph Smith, and they soon began what was to be a remarkable odyssey. The Mormons fled first to Ohio, then to Missouri, and finally to Illinois. At each stop they faced enormous hostility, but they also picked up growing numbers of converts.

Smith was said to have performed some sensational healings, and he warned with increasing urgency that Judgment Day was at hand. By the time the Mormons had reached Nauvoo, Illinois, the Prophet, as Smith was now generally known, had surrounded himself with a well-disciplined and well-armed legion of followers. His pronouncements began to sound more like those of a new religion and were less obviously Christian. He proclaimed himself King in the Kingdom of God, and even announced his candidacy for president of the United States in 1844.

The word "cult" was not widely used in the mid-nineteenth century, but a man who followed Joseph Smith's path would surely be labeled a "cult leader" today. The hostility and fear provoked by Smith and his followers far surpass any reaction to any modern cult. A quick and easy way to get an idea of how many nineteenth-century people felt about the Mormons is to read *A Study in Scarlet*, first of the famous Sherlock Holmes stories. The origins of the crime that the great detective solves are in Mormon history. The Mormons are viewed as exotic and utterly evil. Arthur Conan Doyle, creator of Sherlock Holmes, was no religious bigot; he was merely reflecting the commonly held view of his time.

Joseph Smith, who had been tarred and feathered in Missouri, was murdered by a mob in Illinois on June 27, 1844.

The death of a founder, particularly one believed by his followers to be divinely inspired, is a moment of

extreme crisis for any religious movement. Most do not survive. The Mormons did. Their new leader, Brigham Young, was a man of enormous skill, energy, and toughness. He led thousands of Mormons on a difficult trek to Utah. There, in what was then wilderness, they established a virtually autonomous, church-run state.

Today Utah is just another state. While its politics still tend to be dominated by Mormons, no one feels, upon entering Utah, that they have left the United States.

Over the past century, the fear and hatred with which the vast majority of Americans once viewed the Mormons have almost entirely disappeared. Mormon missionaries who come knocking at doors are not attacked as they probably would have been a century ago. Of course, the Mormons, too, have changed. Many of the practices and beliefs that set them so far out of mainstream society have been softened or abandoned. Most notably, the Mormon practice of polygamy, or plural marriage, was finally ended in about 1890 for most Mormons.

While the heartland of the Mormons is still Utah, the church has millions of members worldwide and an enormous missionary effort. There is a very definite hierarchy among the Mormons, but they can no longer be considered a rigidly disciplined and monolithic group that owes total allegiance to a single leader, any more than the Roman Catholic Church can. Certainly no one today would think of referring to the Mormons as a cult.

THIS ENGRAVING DEPICTS THE DEATH OF JOSEPH SMITH, FOUNDER OF THE MORMON CHURCH.

THE LUBAVITCHERS

Can the world "cult" be applied to the Lubavitcher Hasidim? The Hasidic (or Chasidic) movement began among the Jews of Poland in the late eighteenth century. It is a mystical and emotional doctrine that contrasted sharply with the more scholarly and legalistic forms of Judaism, and at first it was regarded with great hostility by the leaders of the more conventional branches of Judaism.

Hasidism was never a single, unified movement. Local groups tended to gather around a leader who was often regarded as having near-miraculous powers. The movement had its ups and downs during the nineteenth and early twentieth centuries. During the Nazi period its central European base was virtually exterminated. But some Hasidic groups had fled to the United States, where they survived and flourished.

Among those groups were the Lubavitchers. The name comes from the central European city where the group began. The group is now centered in Brooklyn, New York.

Like other Hasidic groups, and indeed like certain Christian groups such as the Amish, the Lubavitchers retain the dress and customs of a much earlier era. Lubavitcher communities are tightly knit, and while they may live in the midst of a big city, the average Lubavitcher interacts with outsiders as infrequently as possible.

CHIEF RABBI SCHNEERSON APPEARING BEFORE HIS FOLLOWERS AT THE LUBAVITCH SECT'S WORLD HEADQUARTERS IN BROOKLYN, NEW YORK.

Because their roots go back for well over a century, the Lubavitcher Hasidim were always referred to as a "movement" rather than a "cult," even by those who disapproved of them. However, in recent years that perception has begun to change.

For many years the Lubavitchers have been led by Rabbi Menachem Schneerson, usually referred to by his followers as the Rebbe. Under the Rebbe's leadership the Lubavitchers have grown enormously. The Lubavitchers maintain a strong presence in Israel, and there are Lubavitcher communities throughout the United States and in many other countries. But the center of the movement unquestionably remains the Rebbe's home in Brooklyn.

Many outside of the Hasidic world have wondered why the leader of this deeply religious Jewish group has not moved to the Jewish state of Israel. The reason is that the Lubavitchers and some other very orthodox Jewish groups do not approve of Israel because it is a secular state. It is their view that a Jewish state can be established only by the Messiah. The Rebbe said that he would go to Israel when the Messiah came. There were indications he believed that it would be soon, for his followers in Israel built an exact replica of his Brooklyn headquarters for him to live in when the great day came.

Then slowly, during the 1980s and early 1990s, the belief grew among a segment of the Lubavitchers that Rabbi Menachem Schneerson himself was the Messiah. The Rebbe never "revealed himself" or announced that he was the Messiah. On the other hand, he did nothing to discourage those who claimed he was, and he could have stopped them cold with just a few words. By 1992 the messianic excitement among the Lubavitchers had reached an almost frenzied pitch. Some expected the Rebbe to "reveal himself" at any moment. Followers put up billboards and placed full-page newspaper ads with large pictures of the Rebbe and announcements that the Messiah was coming.

That got the attention of the outside world. Previously, the Lubavitchers, when they were noticed at all by the media, were usually treated very respectfully. After the messianic excitement the treatment was less respectful, and the word "cult" began to creep into discussions of what had previously always been called the Lubavitcher "movement." With the belief that its leader was not merely divinely inspired, but actually divine, the Lubavitchers crossed a line in public perception.

The future of the Lubavitchers seemed highly uncertain after the Rebbe, who was over ninety, suffered a serious stroke and died in 1994. For months before his death, his medical condition was a closely held secret, but the best guess was that he was completely debilitated and unable to make his wishes known to those who were caring for him. He had no designated successor. The fact that he had never named a successor was one reason some came to believe he was the Messiah, for then no successor would be necessary. How the Lubavitchers will survive the death of so central a figure—or even if they will at all—only time will tell.

A MEDICAL CULT

While the word "cult" most commonly is applied to religious groups, political, scientific, and medical theories have often developed followings that can properly be described as cultlike. Take the curious case of Dr. Wilhelm Reich. Dr. Reich was a brilliant and influential medical man. He was an early disciple of Sigmund Freud, the founder of psychoanalysis. During the 1920s and 1930s, Reich was nearly as well known as his famous mentor. At some point Reich came to believe that he had discovered a previously unknown form of energy that he called "orgone energy." This energy, he said, came from the sun and was present in all organic matter. Proper distribution of this energy was essential to human health. By 1940 he had developed what came to be called an orgone box, an ordinary looking wooden box with an inner layer of metal that was supposed to accumulate orgone energy. A person who sat in it, or used one of the other orgone-accumulating devices that poured out of Reich's laboratory, could be cured of a variety of diseases, including some forms of cancer.

Thousands of sick people who were getting no help from conventional treatments were attracted to Reich's theories. His Institute of Orgonomy, located on Long Island, New York, was filled by his most devoted followers, most of whom were both well-to-do and well educated. The institute took on a genuine cultlike atmosphere.

Reich's ideas got nuttier and nuttier. He said that hostile flying saucers were stealing the earth's orgone energy and that Christ had been in direct communication with cosmic orgone forces. In his book *Listen, Little Man!* he denounced all those who failed to recognize his genius as small-minded fools. He claimed that the medical establishment and the government had conspired to suppress his theories.

In the end, it was not his ideas but his selling and renting of orgone-accumulating devices that were supposed to cure diseases that got him into trouble with the U.S. Food and Drug Administration. He ignored injunctions and finally was brought to trial, convicted, and sentenced to two years in jail. He died there in 1957, after serving less than half his sentence. Wilhelm Reich was no simple medical quack out to fleece his followers by selling them phony cures. He genuinely believed his grandiose theories. Had he been insincere he could easily have avoided jail. In the eyes of his devoted followers he died a martyr's death. A small coterie of believers in Reich's orgone theories still exists.

As we can see from these three very different examples, the answer to the question, "What is a cult?" is not easy to determine.

Though we cannot arrive at a brief, dictionary-style definition, there are a number of particular characteristics we should look for:

1. A group of people is devoted to a particular set of beliefs or ideas, or to a particular individual—usually both.

2. The set of beliefs or the leader is absolutely central to the lives of the group members, more important than any other beliefs or person.

3. The group is usually fairly small. Some cults have had thousands of adherents, but not millions; most have a hard-core membership of under one thousand. The larger the group the more likely it is to become fragmented.

4. Members of the group tend to be isolated from the rest of society. This is obvious in groups like those led by David Koresh and Jim Jones—members of the groups lived in colonies or compounds physically isolated from others. Some cults, however, have existed in the middle of large cities, or have had members scattered throughout the world. In such cases cult members tend to have all their primary relationships with other cult members rather than with members of their families, co-workers, neighbors, or other outsiders.

5. Cults are generally both millennial and apocalyptic. They see the world on the verge of great change. On the one hand, they promise the imminent triumph of their own particular ideology; on the other, they see the world rushing headlong toward cataclysmic destruction. Commonly, both views are held simultaneously. A belief in gradual or evolutionary change is rarely part of cult thinking. Typically, a cult is in a constant state of excitement while awaiting imminent world-shaking events and new revelations.

6. While cult leaders claim near godlike wisdom and power, they also see themselves and their followers as being horribly persecuted by an evil outside world.

7. Cult philosophy or doctrine is usually all-inclusive; it explains just about everything and ties all apparently random events in the world and in the life of the individual member into a neat and satisfying package. Virtually every major news event can be related to the core cult belief.

8. Cults tend to be fairly short-lived; only a tiny percentage survive the passing of their leader, and many dissolve long before that. Cults that survive into the second or third generation of leadership usually do

not remain cults. They modify their philosophy and behavior to bring them more in line with the outside world.

9. For a group to be regarded as a cult, its doctrines and activities must be thought of as not only strange but potentially dangerous. Cults are often believed to have some hidden or secret and thoroughly evil doctrine.

10. Finally, cults are widely believed to possess extraordinary powers of mind control, an ability to capture the innocent and reduce them to near mindless automatons.

MIND CONTROL

The sight of people blindly following obviously insane leaders like David Koresh or Jim Jones, even to their deaths, is what most puzzles and frightens people about cults.

Do these groups or their leaders possess some special, even supernatural, power to control the minds of their followers? In any discussion of cults, terms like hypnotism, mind control, brainwashing, programming, even possession, inevitably arise.

The language may be new but the concerns are ancient, and so are the problems of deciding what is going on. Take, for example, the group that is known to us as the Assassins. The Assassins were a small breakaway group of Shia Muslims that began in Persia late in the eleventh century under the leadership of Hasan bin Sabbah. In 1090, Hasan and his followers captured the great and nearly impregnable fortress of Alamut, or

Eagle's Nest. From there his influence spread through large portions of what is now Iran, Iraq, and Syria.

Then, as now, the political and religious situation in that part of the world was both complex and violent. The Assassins were only one of a large number of cults or sects. What has given them their sinister fame is the suicidally fanatic devotion that Hasan is said to have inspired in his followers.

A PERSIAN MANUSCRIPT ILLUSTRATION
SHOWING (AT RIGHT) HASAN BIN SABBAH,
FOUNDER OF THE ASSASSINS.

One typical account appeared in several European chronicles. A visitor to Alamut was standing on the ramparts of the castle with Hasan. The leader pointed to a white-robed guard standing on a turret nearby. "You see that devotee standing guard," said Hasan. "Watch!" He made a signal with his hand, and the man instantly threw up his hands in salute and jumped from the turret to his death. Scenes based on this story have made their way into countless popular novels and films. However, as with many of the most sensational accounts of the group, there is no way of determining if it is true.

The Assassins were fighting the Turks, who had conquered much of the area. They were not powerful enough to confront Turkish might directly, but they did send out fanatic devotees to murder high Turkish officials and others that Hasan regarded as enemies. While murderers were often successful, they were almost always killed during or shortly after their deeds. How was Hasan able to inspire his followers to such suicidal acts?

The name Assassin comes from the Arabic *hash-shashin*, meaning "users of hashish." It was certainly not a name that Hasan's followers called themselves, but when one of Hasan's knife-wielding followers suicidally flung himself on a well-guarded official, it seemed to onlookers that he was crazed with drugs—nothing else could explain the insane act.

Another of the many stories told about the group is that young initiates were drugged and taken to a secret garden near the castle. When they regained consciousness they found themselves in an exquisite setting of flowers, fruit trees, fountains, and golden pavilions. There were also beautiful women who would satisfy every desire. All of this stood in sharp contrast to ordinary life at Alamut, which was spartan and puritanical.

After several days amid this undreamed-of luxury and pleasure, the initiates were again drugged and returned to their ordinary lives. They were told that they had had a brief foretaste of paradise. If they died in the service of their chief and their religion, they would spend all eternity in such bliss.

This exotic tale has been repeated endlessly, but, like so many good stories, it seems to have no basis in fact. Indeed, there is no evidence that the Assassins ever used drugs for any purpose. The name Hashshashin was applied to them only in later ages by those who had no direct knowledge of their practices. It is most likely that Hasan bin Sabbah employed no artificial means to inspire the fanatic devotion of his followers. It is so difficult for outsiders to understand this degree of devotion that we tend to credit practically any story that seems to explain it.

When the word "assassin" first entered European languages, it meant "devotee." Only later did it pick up its present-day meaning of political murderer.

Devotees of many other religions and philosophies— from the Zealots of ancient Israel to the Christian martyrs of Rome to the members of today's Irish Republican Army—have faced, and even courted, horrible deaths or done other things in the service of their beliefs that seem utterly against all reason and humanity.

The question is not whether people will act in ways most others consider extreme or insane for a particular leader or set of beliefs—of course they will. The question is whether they do so voluntarily. That is not easy to decide. And most often the answer depends on whether or not we agree with what is being done.

During the witch persecutions of the sixteenth and seventeenth centuries, thousands of individuals confessed "voluntarily" to flying around on broomsticks and doing a lot of other things that, quite simply, never happened. Since most of the confessions were made after torture or under the threat of torture, we would not consider them voluntary. But to those who were conducting the witchcraft trials, voluntary meant that the individuals were not actually being tortured at the moment the confession was made. Johan Weyer, an early opponent of the witchcraft persecutions, commented, "We are not all witches, because we have not all been tortured."

Yet there is something about these confessions that should give us pause. A certain percentage of people did hold beliefs or engage in practices that orthodox religious authorities regarded as witchcraft. Some of these practices may have involved the use of drugs, such as belladonna, capable of causing hallucinations. Thus, when an individual confessed to flying around on a broomstick, she (most witchcraft accusations were brought against women) may have been describing a drug-induced hallucination.

But more significant for our discussion is the possibility that people who engaged in none of these practices still became convinced of their guilt. Accused as well as accusers believed in the possibility of witchcraft. If persons of authority hammered at them day after day with the charge that they had committed certain acts, then it is quite possible that the weaker and more suggestible became convinced that they had indeed done such things. Why would God allow them to suffer so if they were not guilty? Thus, they might have confessed not merely to spare themselves further torture, but because they had come to share their accusers' fantasies. In a sense one might conclude they had been "programmed" to confess. As we will see in Chapter 6, this can still happen in the latter part of the twentieth century.

HYPNOTISM AND CONDITIONING

The use of hypnotism opened the possibility of a more subtle and pervasive kind of mind control. The public was fascinated by the fictional figures of the evil hypnotist Svengali and his helpless subject Trilby, by the murderous somnambulist of the silent film *The Cabinet of Dr. Caligari*, and by the murderous automatons of a thousand lesser books and films. Few authorities on hypnosis believe that the hypnotist can exercise anything remotely resembling this sort of control over a subject, but the public perception was, and still is, that such control is possible. Anguished parents of cult members often say that their sons or daughters have been "hypnotized" by the cult leader.

The next step in the development of mind control—or at least in the popular image of mind control—came with the work of the Russian psychologist Ivan Pavlov. Pavlov was able to condition laboratory animals to produce certain involuntary responses. For example, a dog could be conditioned to salivate when a bell was rung.

THE SPELL CAST BY THE EVIL SVENGALI
OVER THE BEAUTIFUL YOUNG TRILBY HAS
COME TO SYMBOLIZE THE EVIL POTENTIAL OF
HYPNOTISM AS A MEANS OF GAINING TOTAL
POWER OVER ANOTHER HUMAN BEING.

Pavlov's work raised the possibility—or more accurately, the suspicion—that voluntary functions could be conditioned in a similar manner. That, for example, a person could be "conditioned" to recite a certain speech against his or her will whenever a bell was rung.

Pavlov was a long way from attempting any such experiments, but his work had a tremendous influence over Soviet psychology—and to Westerners it looked very sinister. The worst fears about "Pavlovian" conditioning appeared to be confirmed during the notorious show trials of the 1930s. The world was treated to the spectacle of old Bolsheviks—men who, hardened by years of revolutionary activity, should have been well beyond caving in under normal threats of torture—parading into court and meekly confessing to absurd and impossible crimes. The same prisoners then went off to their deaths without uttering (as far as we know) a word of criticism of those who had condemned them. The suspicion rose that the Soviets possessed some kind of mysterious "Pavlovian" conditioning techniques that could bend and break the toughest wills.

What really convinced the American public that this sort of mind control was possible was the experience of the Korean War. During the war, a small number of American prisoners of war (POWs) confessed publicly to war crimes and broadcast messages that praised the North Koreans and Chinese and condemned their own countrymen. While such behavior was not welcomed by the American public, people were willing to concede that men would "break" under pressure. The really shocking part came after the war when some of these prisoners refused to come home when offered the opportunity to do so. Even with the direct physical threat removed, it appeared that the Chinese had a powerful hold over their former captives.

The Chinese have a term, *hsi nao*, which means "cleansing the mind." Edward Hunter, who first described in detail the Chinese methods of indoctrinating prisoners, coined the term "brainwashing" for the Chinese technique. The term was both sinister and mysterious, and it stuck.

The image of the nearly supernatural power of brainwashing was reinforced by Richard Condon's extremely popular novel *The Manchurian Candidate* and the 1962 film made from it. It is about a Korean War prisoner who has been turned into a brainwashed zombie programmed to kill a presidential candidate. It was thriller fiction, but the notion that a kind of *Manchurian Candidate* mind control might be possible was taken seriously by many.

When the Chinese techniques were studied closely it turned out that there was nothing mysterious or particularly new about "brainwashing." It consisted of breaking down a person through a combination of physical and mental stress and by constantly repeating the ideas that the captor wished to put across. There was no resort to extreme physical torture, though prisoners were occasionally beaten. The captors depended on more subtle methods—depriving the prisoner of sleep or use of the toilet, serving a uniformly monotonous diet, imposing long periods of isolation, and so on.

When a prisoner was thoroughly broken, a process of "education" began. The prisoner was given more freedom than before, though still subjected to a strict regimen of reading and lectures. After a while the prisoner was encouraged to write or record a confession. The more cooperative the prisoner was the more comforts and privileges were likely to be granted. And over the entire process hung the threat of a return to severe conditions. Ultimately the prisoner became more or less convinced that he or she had not confessed because of weakness, but because of genuinely coming to recognize past errors in his or her life.

The same basic techniques of coercion have been used by police throughout the world to get accused persons to confess, in army training camps to give raw recruits the proper *esprit de corps*, and even in fraternity initiations. The new member is often degraded, harangued, and made to suffer considerable discomfort before he is properly initiated.

And, of course, these techniques have been used by cults. Those who have left cults frequently talk about how they were fed poorly, deprived of sleep, humiliated, and occasionally even beaten. During this period they were subjected to endless sermons and lectures.

From its study of what had happened to Korean War prisoners, the U.S. military learned a great deal. Most significantly it learned that brainwashing techniques were not irresistible. Most prisoners did not confess to war crimes or refuse to return home after the war. Investigators concluded that many of those who did succumb were ill-prepared for the experience of being captured. They were draftees hastily trained for war. The Korean War was unpopular, many of the Americans fighting there did not know why they were fighting. In addition, many of the prisoners had suffered bad experiences in the military and in previous civilian life, and were dissatisfied with both America and the military even before they were captured.

The Korean POW experience was not repeated in Vietnam, though that war was even more unpopular. It may have been because the military was able to better prepare men for what would happen to them if they were captured. But it probably had more to do with the type of prisoners in Vietnam. Most of them were Air Force officers, highly motivated and highly trained professionals. They were not draftees who didn't want to be there in the first place.

The studies have concluded that while brainwashing is a terrible experience and often an effective method of breaking down resistance, there is nothing supernatural about it. The "secret" can be summed up in the bit of folk wisdom that "every man has his breaking point."

But in early 1974, it was hard for a lot of people to believe that there wasn't something supernatural about brainwashing.

PROGRAMMING AND DEPROGRAMMING

On February 5, 1974, a series of events began that focused the attention of the American public on the issue of cult mind control as nothing else has, before or since. On that day Patricia "Patty" Hearst, granddaughter of the famous newspaper publisher William Randolph Hearst, was abducted from her apartment in Berkeley, California.

The kidnappers turned out to be a small and very violent radical group, the Symbionese Liberation Army (SLA), a group that could accurately be described as a political cult. It was led by an escaped convict named Donald DeFreeze, who called himself Marshal Cinque. Two members were already under arrest for the murder of the Oakland, California, school superintendent.

After the kidnapping the SLA made a variety of demands, including the distribution of free food to the poor and the release of other members of the group who were in jail. Taped messages from the kidnap victim urged that the demands be met. She described herself as a "prisoner of war" and said she might be killed if the police threatened her abductors. By early April, however, the nature of the messages from Patty Hearst began to change. She said that she had joined her abductors and been converted to their beliefs. A picture of the young woman holding an automatic weapon and standing in front of the SLA symbol was sent with a message. She now called herself Tania.

The first reaction to this startling communication was that Patty had been forced to record it. But when the SLA robbed a bank in San Francisco on April 15, among the participants in the robbery was an armed Patty Hearst. Some speculated that her weapon was not loaded and that others in the group actually had their weapons trained on her. Her father, Randolph Hearst, said that she had been "brainwashed." More tapes surfaced in which Patty denied she had been "brainwashed" and described herself as a willing participant in the robbery. Many law enforcement officials believed her, and she was declared a "fugitive" rather than a "victim." The conversion from kidnapped heiress to revolutionary terrorist was so dramatic and difficult to accept that there was even speculation that the whole kidnapping had been faked, and that Patty Hearst had been allied with the group before February, but no evidence for that charge ever surfaced.

THE TRANSFORMATION OF THE SWEET YOUNG SOCIALITE, PATTY HEARST, INTO TANIA, THE GUN-WIELDING MEMBER OF THE SLA, WAS HERALDED AS THE PRIME EXAMPLE OF THE POWER OF "BRAINWASHING."

In May, six members of the SLA, including leader DeFreeze, died in a fire that was a result of a wild shoot-out with the police. Patty Hearst and two other SLA members had been in the vicinity but not in the house that the police raided. They escaped, but it was generally assumed that with the core leadership of the tiny radical cult dead, the remaining fugitives would quickly be captured or surrender. Yet weeks, and then months, passed. Despite one of the most intensive police and FBI searches in history, the fugitive heiress and her companions eluded capture. There must have been countless opportunities during this period in which Patty could have fled if she had wished to do so. More tapes surfaced in which the fugitive heiress continued to declare her commitment to the ideals of the SLA. Almost daily, the press was filled with pronouncements about "brainwashing."

Astonishingly, Patty Hearst successfully outwitted the police and FBI for months. During that period she was probably the most famous woman in America. Yet, when she finally was captured it didn't take long for her to renounce her conversion to the SLA terrorist philosophy. She said that after she had been kidnapped she had been locked in a closet for weeks on end, and was regularly abused and subjected to almost unending propaganda. This treatment (which sounded very much like brainwashing) finally worked, she said. Its hold was broken only after she had been captured by the police and essentially "deprogrammed."

The claim that one had been "brainwashed" into committing crimes was not an adequate legal defense. Patty Hearst had unquestionably been involved in serious crimes, most notably bank robbery. She was brought to trial and convicted. However, she served a relatively brief sentence, and after her release slipped back into obscurity.

————

The Patty Hearst case fascinated and frightened an awful lot of people. If the newspaper heiress could be forcibly and rapidly converted into a gun-toting terrorist, was anyone, particularly any young person, safe? It seemed as if *The Manchurian Candidate* did not have to be set in some remote Asian prison camp. Things like that could happen right here in the United States of America.

During the 1970s, anxiety over the possibility of cult brainwashing—or programming, as it was often called—rose markedly. The primary trigger for this fear before the Patty Hearst kidnapping was the rise of what was called the Jesus Movement. The Jesus Movement was a general term for a collection of groups that espoused rigid biblical fundamentalism and often advocated communal lifestyles. No one can really be sure how many of these groups really existed or how many members they had, but a few high-profile groups attracted a great deal of attention.

The more radical cults demanded total commitment from their members. The young converts would leave their families, sometimes never to return. If they did make a brief visit, they would often denounce their parents' lives as "godless," warn them of their eternal damnation, and answer all questions and entreaties with stock biblical passages.

Parents were first baffled and then horrified by this apparent transformation. Attempts to reason with their disaffected sons and daughters just triggered more Bible quotes. Threats and pleas didn't work.

————

Some parents opted for stronger measures. They tried to kidnap their children, some of whom were adults. In a few cases they had their children committed to mental institutions. Often the children simply waited for a chance to escape right back to the community from which they had been "rescued."

The situation was not historically unique. In other eras, children abandoned the beliefs and customs of their parents for a passionate commitment to new and different doctrines. In the past such changes were often called the work of the devil. In the late twentieth century it has been called the result of brainwashing or programming.

If young people could be "programmed," then presumably they could be "deprogrammed." Soon a variety of individuals calling themselves deprogrammers appeared on the scene. The first to gain wide public attention was a former California state official named Ted Patrick. Patrick declared a holy war against some of the more radical Jesus cults. His services were engaged by a number of distraught parents. His activities kept his name in the newspapers, and on several occasions got him arrested. Many of those who Patrick deprogrammed were physically removed from the communes or compounds in which they were living— in short, they were kidnapped. This was always done with the consent and sometimes the assistance of the parents. However, when the cult member being snatched was already of legal age, the act could become a police matter. The police, however, were generally reluctant to get involved, and the general public was more sympathetic to the concerns of parents than to the rights of young cult members.

Some of those who had been kidnapped by Patrick later expressed gratitude to him and to their parents for "saving" them. Others who resisted deprogramming were not so forgiving. But they rarely signed complaints against Patrick, either because their religious communities did not want the publicity or because they would also have to swear out complaints against their own parents. The few times when Patrick was brought to court he was usually acquitted. However, in May 1974 he was convicted of unlawfully imprisoning two young women in Denver.

What is deprogramming? Ted Patrick and others who have followed in his footsteps have generally been vague about explaining their methods. But in 1973, CBS News broadcast a major five-part series on deprogramming that provided the most complete and intimate look at how the technique is supposed to work that we are ever likely to get. Patrick had allowed CBS to film some, but not all, of the attempted deprogramming of a twenty-year-old girl.

The filmed sessions consisted primarily of Patrick hammering away at the young convert's beliefs for hours on end. There were some highly emotional moments when the girl's parents were brought in. The series made Patrick and deprogramming look bad, which is probably why other cult deprogrammers will not invite the cameras in to film them at work. Patrick must have realized how bad his methods looked because at one point he ordered the cameraman out entirely. Many viewers, even those who strongly disliked cults, reacted with delight when they heard that the girl, after having been declared successfully deprogrammed, grabbed the first opportunity to run away and return to the group from which she had been taken.

Civil liberties lawyers interviewed for the series insisted that Patrick's methods were illegal because the girl was of legal age and being held against her will. Yet police authorities would not intervene, even while she was being carried off, protesting loudly, right before their eyes and right in front of television cameras.

There was no evidence of actual physical coercion in the deprogramming process, if you can ignore the fact that the girl was being held against her will. The girl's parents seemed to think of deprogramming as a sort of exorcism. They spoke of demons being expelled from their daughter's body. In the Denver, Colorado, case, two young women said that Patrick accused them of being "zombies" and "possessed by the devil."

Ted Patrick and other deprogrammers have claimed great success for their methods. There are testimonials from young people who say that they have been "saved" by the intervention of a deprogrammer. But there is no hard evidence that these methods are particularly effective, and in some cases they may make matters worse. Deprogrammers are often able to pry large fees out of anxious and desperate parents with promises that their children will be "returned" to them.

With the decline of the Jesus Movement, public and media interest in programming and deprogramming slipped. That did not mean the practices disappeared. For years a sort of underground war has been fought, on the streets and in the courts, between cults and parents or other relatives of cult members, aided by a shadowy group of deprogrammers operating on or beyond the fringes of the law. Then, in the early 1990s, another case involving a member of a rich and prominent family moved the subject back onto the front pages.

THE LAROUCHIES

Sometime in the mid-1980s, Lewis du Pont Smith, a member of one of America's richest and most powerful families, became involved with the followers of Lyndon LaRouche. The LaRouchies, as they are often called, hotly deny that they are a cult, and they do not display many of the characteristics traditionally associated with the popular notion of a cult. They are not a religious group, or a political one in any traditional sense. LaRouche's followers do not all live in a particular compound or commune. Far from seeking to cut themselves off from the outside world, they engage the world actively, even aggressively.

In a lengthy 1993 article on Lewis du Pont Smith and the LaRouche group, the magazine *Vanity Fair* quotes a woman who spent fifteen years close to the group's center of power. "There is no question it's a cult," she said. "The thing that defines a cult is that it creates a reality within itself that bears little resemblance to reality outside." She added that it is important to remember "One big kahuna runs the whole show. It's a shared delusion."

The Lyndon LaRouche philosophy is hard to pin down. According to LaRouche, the world is controlled by a variety of interlocking conspiratorial groups that are leading us all to destruction, a fate from which only LaRouche can save us. One of the LaRouche theories is that the Queen of England is head of the worldwide drug trade. Though the villains and plots shift with the times, the sense of secret control and impending doom are constant. Those who follow LaRouche are given a sense of mission and a feeling of superiority. They, and they alone, know what is really going on in the world. The rest of us are deluded fools, or worse, agents of the conspiracy.

There are perhaps a thousand hard-core LaRouche followers scattered throughout the United States and Europe. They control a variety of organizations and publications, and the LaRouche affiliation is often, though not always, hidden. Perhaps the most sinister aspect of the LaRouche network is the obsessive way that members gather information about those they regard as enemies—and that could be practically anyone. They have also been used by other organizations and governments to dig up and disseminate hostile, and often totally untrue, tales about individuals and groups.

LaRouche regularly ran for the presidency of the United States. He never received more than a relative handful of votes, but he did buy lots of television time to expound some of his less nutty theories as part of his campaign. LaRouche-backed candidates also frequently enter local elections, and on a few occasions have actually won minor contests when they kept their affiliation hidden.

The LaRouche organization is expensive to run, and the source of their funds is murky. They are tenacious fund-raisers, and in the view of U.S. authorities some of their practices are downright illegal. Lyndon LaRouche himself was convicted of fraud and tax evasion and given a fifteen-year jail sentence, but he was able to control his followers effectively from behind bars. In January, 1994, LaRouche was paroled after serving five years. He expressed no regrets and said he would continue to head his organization.

Political extremist Lyndon LaRouche (right) departs
the Federal Courthouse in Alexandria, Virginia, after
denying federal fraud and conspiracy charges.

Because he was wealthy (he inherited an estimated $10 million), Lewis duPont Smith became the LaRouchies' prime convert. LaRouche himself, before he was sent to jail, was best man at Lewis's wedding to another of his followers.

Despite the fact that Lewis is not a minor (he was almost thirty when he became involved in the LaRouche group), his family has waged a determined, expensive, and very public campaign to get him out of the cult they believe has brainwashed him. Lots of families have tried to get their children out of cults, but few, if any, have had the resources of the duPont Smiths at their command.

His parents have had Lewis declared incompetent to handle his financial affairs, and thus severely restricted his ability to give money to LaRouche. This act, however, seemed to drive Lewis deeper into the LaRouche group. His father, Edgar Newbold Smith, finally hired a deprogrammer named Galen Kelly. Kelly, who claims to have successfully deprogrammed hundreds of cult members, told the *Vanity Fair* reporter that he had no apologies for his activities. "Have there been occasions when I've taken people forcibly, involuntarily? Yes. If you want to call it kidnapping, call it kidnapping," he said.

The problem was that Lewis—six feet tall, two hundred and twenty five pounds, thirty-six years old, and a former wrestling champ—was no kid. And he was usually surrounded by other LaRouchies. Edgar Smith then enlisted the services of some former deputy sheriffs, who tried to devise a way to snatch Lewis and hide him away somewhere until he could be deprogrammed. Unfortunately for the plotters, one of the former deputies went to a LaRouche lawyer and then to the FBI. He was given a recording device to wear and was able to record some sixty hours of discussion of strange, often laughable, kidnapping plots. Then the FBI arrested Edgar Smith, Kelly, and two others for conspiracy to kidnap.

A sensational trial that involved not only a secretive cult but one of America's wealthiest families naturally attracted a great deal of attention. With teams of competing psychiatrists and representatives of groups like the Cult Awareness Network (CAN), an anticult group financed by angry relatives, and the Deprogramming Survivors Network, which is controlled by the Church of Scientology, a group many consider a cult, the trial gave the public a look at the shadow war that is being waged over cults.

Though the evidence confirmed that Edgar Newbold Smith had discussed a plan to kidnap his son with a group of men who were certainly capable of attempting such an act, the jury found them all not guilty. Juries frequently side with families in cases like this. And they may not have taken the plot very seriously. The judge had called the defendants "the gang that couldn't shoot straight."

After the verdict, the judge pleaded with father and son to reconcile. He said that nothing in life was more important than a son's relationship to his father. As with so many families split by cult membership, this plea for reason didn't work.

Satanic Cults

It is difficult enough to determine whether or not a group should properly be called a cult. With satanic cults there is another layer of difficulty. It must first be determined whether the group exists at all.

There are few subjects in America today that inspire as much fear and fascination as satanic cults. And few subjects are more controversial. Some people, particularly fundamentalist Christians, hold that any group that is avowedly non-Christian, or at least non-monotheistic, is really satanic. In the past, Christian missionaries confronting unfamiliar religious beliefs often assumed that the people were worshiping demons. Today groups like the Hari Krishna, which has its roots in the Hindu religion, and most New Age groups, have been called satanic.

More commonly, those who call themselves witches or modern pagans are denounced as satanic.

This is an accusation that today's witches hotly deny, and we'll look at that subject more closely in Chapter 7. For the present we will confine ourselves to groups that actually do worship Satan, the devil, or whatever we wish to call the principle of evil.

————

Logically, Satanism should not exist; indeed it cannot exist. Satanism has been called the reverse of Christianity. This definition, however, presents an insoluble problem. The Christian devil is not an evil god. He is not a god at all. In the Old Testament, Satan is just another servant of God, one created as an instrument of temptation and punishment. The struggle between God and Satan is in a sense a sham, since Satan is never out of God's control, and his defeat is inevitable.

Thus, to worship Satan is to worship not a powerful and independent figure of evil, but a servant who has an unpleasant task to perform but no real power to grant any favors. To worship the biblical Satan is to condemn oneself to eternal damnation.

Of course, it's not that simple; it never is. Neither Judaism nor Christianity developed or existed in a religious vacuum. There were other highly influential sects and movements that saw the world as the battleground between two forces of equal or nearly equal strength—one good, the other evil. And the triumph of good was not necessarily a foregone conclusion. Most influential were the Manichaeans. Manichaeism developed into a sophisticated body of religious thought that was both influenced by Christianity and attractive to many Christians. No less a figure than Saint Augustine had at one time been a Manichaean. The Manichaeans were not devil worshipers or fol-

————

lowers of the principle of evil. Actually they were generally more ascetic and rigid than Christians of the time. But they did recognize the possibility of competing yet equal forces of good and evil, and such a belief is a necessity if one is to become a devil worshiper.

Manichaeism was declared a dangerous heresy, and the various sects and cults it inspired were persecuted with ruthless vigor. As far as most official histories are concerned, the belief was wiped out in the West in about the sixth century. But many think that Manichaean beliefs continued to flourish underground for centuries, perhaps even to the present day. Discussions of modern Satanism often trace its origins back to the Manichaeans.

It is also possible to read the New Testament and come away with the distinct impression that Satan possesses a good measure of independent power. Perhaps he is not an equal of God, but he sometimes appears supreme on Earth and is able to grant those who follow him earthly rewards. Christian theologians denied this, but most common folk were less interested in theology than in simply getting through life. The appeal of a readily accessible, though evil, earthly monarch as contrasted to an awesome, but distant and perhaps indifferent, supreme God must have been great. Many sincere Christians undoubtedly felt desperate enough to risk eternal damnation in order to gain some measure of success in this world. Others felt that

A POWERFULLY WICKED AND VIVIDLY
IMAGINATIVE SCENE DEPICTING SATAN
PRESIDING OVER SABBATH SERVICES.

through the use of magical formulas they could force the devil and his demonic hosts to do their bidding, and still not pay the eternal price. Or they even believed that it wasn't really wrong to ask the devil for earthly rewards, so long as one also paid attention to spiritual duties, such as attending mass regularly. Today many good Christians also consult their astrological charts and feel no basic conflict, though such forms of divination are expressly forbidden in the Bible.

The obstacles to deciding whether or not there ever was a large and organized satanic movement are formidable. Surviving records from the early days of Christianity through the end of the Middle Ages are almost exclusively church records. These documents describe the activities of a variety of "satanic" or "diabolical" groups. But how are such records to be interpreted? The Church habitually regarded all non-Christians, as well as many Christians with whom it disagreed, as devil worshipers. Pagans, heretics, Jews, and Muslims were all indiscriminately labeled devil worshipers at one time or another. All were accused of a variety of abominable practices, from copulating with the devil to sacrificing unbaptized infants. The Roman Catholic Church accused early Protestants of being servants of the devil, and Protestants returned the accusation with interest. In such an atmosphere it is difficult to decide whether groups were diabolical, simply different, or entirely imaginary.

It is quite likely that there were some organized groups in genuine revolt against the rigid structure of orthodox Christianity. As a sign of that revolt they may have paid homage to the devil, defied traditional morality, and performed perverted versions of Christian rituals. But the available evidence indicates that if such groups existed at all, they were neither numerous nor well organized. They drew their support largely from the desperate poor.

More glamorous were groups like the Hellfire Club of eighteenth-century England. The Hellfire Club was typical of many groups labeled satanic. It consisted of wealthy, bored young gentlemen who met to dabble in magic, hold orgies, and generally outrage the respectable establishment. They often dressed in monks' robes and performed obscene parodies of Christian rituals. Most then went on to lead perfectly respectable lives as members of the British upper class. Two interesting names have been associated with the Hellfire Club. The first is John Wilkes, a radical politician who was the only supporter of American independence in the British Parliament at the time of the Revolution. Wilkes was very popular in America. The second is Benjamin Franklin, who reputedly attended meetings of The Hellfire Club while he was in England. This allegation cannot be proved, but it is not implausible, for Franklin was neither a practicing Christian nor a moral puritan, though he did not personally like the radical Wilkes.

The popular modern picture of Satanism, black mass and all, is drawn more from literary sources than from history. The most influential is *La-Bas* (*Down There*) by the late-nineteenth-century French writer J.K. Huysmans. Huysmans's descriptions of satanic practices, including the black mass, were supposed to have been based on the activities of a group actually operating in Paris when he wrote. Huysmans was well acquainted with a variety of occult groups and societies of his day, but *La-Bas* is a work of imaginative fiction, not journalism.

TWENTIETH-CENTURY SATANISM

A name that crops up regularly in any discussion of modern Satanism is Aleister Crowley, an early-twentieth-century British occultist who has been called "the wickedest man in the world." Despite that title, which he quite enjoyed, Crowley never considered himself a Satanist, for he believed in neither God nor the devil. He did try to practice magic. Crowley was a drug addict, a drunkard, a sadist, a monumental egotist, and a publicity-seeking screwball. For years his well-reported exploits alternately titillated and shocked readers of sensational newspapers and magazines throughout the world.

For all his notoriety, Crowley really never had much of a following. But he was a prolific writer, and many of the agonizingly long chants and rituals he devised are now pointed to as being Satanist liturgy. Crowley was very likely the model for the chief Satanist in Ira Levin's novel *Rosemary's Baby*.

It's difficult to figure out when, or even if, Crowley was serious, for he had a nasty sense of humor, and after he ran through his personal fortune was forced to live by his wits. That involved peddling a lot of esoteric and magical hokum.

Many of those who today consider themselves experts on Satanism invoke Crowley's works and par-

NINETEENTH-CENTURY FRENCH WRITER
J. K. HUYSMANS'S DESCRIPTION OF SATANISM
IN HIS BOOK PROVIDES US WITH MANY OF
THE MYTHICAL IDEAS OF HOW SATANISTS
ACTUALLY CARRY OUT THEIR RITUALS.

THOUGH ALEISTER CROWLEY NEVER HAD MUCH OF A PERSONAL FOLLOWING DURING HIS LIFETIME, HIS INFLUENCE ON MODERN OCCULTISM IS ENORMOUS.

ticularly his statement: "Do what thou wilt shall be the whole of the law." This is supposed to be the ultimate satanic justification for anything, including murder. Though Aleister Crowley wasn't a very deep thinker, he wasn't all that simpleminded, either. In his *Book of the Law*, Crowley indicates that he was a believer in destiny and "do what thou wilt" did not simply mean "do what you like" but rather "live in harmony with your destiny." Actually it is pointless to spend a lot of time trying to figure out what Crowley meant, for he often said that even *he* didn't understand all of it.

The best-known Satanist group of modern times is the Church of Satan, which was headed by a one-time carnival worker named Anton Szandor LaVey. The organization was anything but a secretive cult. LaVey sought publicity and usually got it, granting interviews to any reporter he could buttonhole. Started in 1966, the Church of Satan grew out of small informal classes in occultism that LaVey had been teaching in San Francisco. It first came to public notice when movie actress Jayne Mansfield joined LaVey's group. LaVey had a dispute with her boyfriend, and when both were killed in an automobile accident the rumor spread that LaVey had "cursed" them. LaVey modestly claimed that he had only cursed the boyfriend.

LaVey got his biggest boost when he was tapped to serve as "technical adviser" and bit-part player in the 1968 film version of *Rosemary's Baby*. As had Crowley, LaVey depended heavily on the popular media of the time for his survival.

At its height, the Church of Satan boasted of having well over 10,000 members, though the accuracy of such a statistic is impossible to determine. LaVey's *Satanic Bible*, first published in 1969, remains an occult best-seller today. In his prime, LaVey was a striking figure with a shaved head and pointed black Vandyke beard. He presided over Church of Satan ceremonies wearing a black cape and a skullcap fitted out with horns. The ceremonies were highly theatrical, with the robed devotees and a nude woman serving as the altar. Bells were rung, and LaVey walked around chanting and waving a sword.

The nude woman as altar is a standard feature of the infamous black mass, which is more of a literary than a religious creation. The sword, the bells, and the rest are drawn from various occult ceremonies. There is, however, one basic flaw in the ritual; it is all window dressing, for Anton LaVey did not believe in the devil.

To LaVey and his followers Satan was not a supernatural being, merely a symbol of the desire for self-gratification that exists in all of us. This, said LaVey, is our "true nature," and it was the purpose of his church to recognize this, not to worship evil.

The Church of Satan was certainly anti-Christian, for according to LaVey, Christianity perverts our "true nature." His theology, such as it is, consists of upside-down Christianity. "Blessed are the strong, for they shall possess the earth. If a man smite you on one cheek, SMASH him on the other!" he wrote in the *Satanic Bible*.

"We recognize," LaVey said, "that man is sometimes lower than the animals, that he is basically greedy and selfish, so why feel guilty about it? We accept ourselves as we are and live with it. The one great sin is self-deceit." This satanic philosophy was not so very different from the "greed is good" philosophy that enjoyed some vogue during the 1980s.

LaVey wasn't interested in the afterlife or eternal damnation. It was the here and now that interested him. Indeed, he was absolutely scornful of those who believe in the supernatural, evil or otherwise.

However, the Church of Satan was not entirely materialist, for it did hold that each individual possesses some sort of internal power with which nature can be bent to his or her will. That, rather than providing good photo opportunities, was supposed to be the purpose of all the rituals and magical trappings. LaVey saw the power as some sort of natural biological force, even though there is absolutely no evidence that such

ANTON LaVEY, ENIGMATIC LEADER OF THE CHURCH OF SATAN.

a force exists. LaVey's view was very close to that of Aleister Crowley and is quite common in modern occult circles.

There was nothing of the civil lawbreaker in LaVey's brand of Satanism. On the contrary, LaVey (who said he had once been a policeman) was politically conservative and an outspoken proponent of law and order. He said, "We have a very clean slate. We are very evil outlaws in theological circles, but not in civil." In this respect, Anton LaVey was far more mainstream than Aleister Crowley, who got into serious trouble with the law in several countries.

Membership in the Church of Satan did appear to be quite respectable in a very conventional way. It ran heavily to professional military men, policemen, technicians, and low-level executives. LaVey claimed that applicants were carefully screened to weed out "nuts" and "losers"—that is, people who were not financially successful.

Drugs, while not specifically condemned by the Church of Satan, were viewed with extreme disfavor, for they cause a "loss of control." There was a great deal of verbal violence in Church of Satan services, but physical violence was not openly advocated. While LaVey discussed human sacrifice in his *Satanic Bible*, he was not talking about actually going out and killing anyone. He wrote, "The use of a human sacrifice in a Satanic ritual does not imply that the sacrifice is slaughtered 'to appease the gods.' *Symbolically*, the victim is destroyed through the working of a hex or curse, which in turn leads to the physical, mental or emotional destruction of the 'sacrifice' in ways not attributable to the magician." Church of Satan services often ended with the whole congregation sitting around cursing people.

While sacrifices of children and animals are said to be regular parts of satanic ritual, LaVey professed to be horrified by such acts. Satanists, he said, are the only ones who possess real respect for life and the human body. Children and animals are entirely "natural" and "unhypocritical" and thus in the view of the Church of Satan are "natural Satanists" not to be sacrificed but protected.

A Satanist should sacrifice, by symbolic means, of course, "anyone who has unjustly wronged you—one who has 'gone out of his way' to hurt you—to deliberately cause trouble and hardship for you or those dear to you. In short, a person, who is asking to be cursed by their very actions." The saying "Don't get mad, get even!" comes to mind.

The possibility that someone might misinterpret the Church of Satan's "human sacrifice" doctrine and actually go out and physically kill or hurt another was dismissed by group members. Anything, they said, could be misinterpreted. They would then go on to name some of the wars that had been conducted in the name of "the Prince of Peace."

There has always been a suspicion that the Church of Satan was nothing more than a money-making scheme cooked up by an old-time carnival con man. LaVey never made any bones about the fact that he made money—lots of it—from his creation. After all, he argued, that is what Satanism is all about. How can you accuse someone of taking your money under false pretenses when he says all along that what he wants to do is take your money?

During the early 1970s, a group called the Process acquired a very sinister satanic reputation. Among other things, they were said to have influenced the murderous Charles Manson and his "family," a charge that members of the Process hotly denied and for which no evidence was ever presented.

The Process had begun in England during the mid-1960s as a sort of therapy group gathered around a charismatic and handsome young architect named Robert de Grimston Moor (eventually known simply as Robert de Grimston). The group began to develop a rather complex and murky theology, apparently based on de Grimston's visions and dreams. Then about thirty members left their careers and their homeland to retire to a small Mexican fishing village and develop their ideas. That lasted about a year. Then the group moved to the United States, where it began to attract attention and new converts.

Even at its height the Process was not a large group, but it appeared to be a very well-financed one. It had headquarters in a number of American and Canadian cities, with a large center in a high-rent building on the Upper East Side of Manhattan. They put out glossy and very attractive publications. The group seemed to attract people with artistic backgrounds as well as some with a good deal of money to throw around.

Like so many cults, they had an apocalyptic vision of the future—the world has to come to an end—and soon. De Grimston wrote, "The distant rumblings that are heralds of the End have become a mighty roar closing in about us, piercing our eardrums and causing the very Earth to quake beneath our feet, so that very soon even the blindest, numbest, most oblivious of us will no longer be able to shut out the sound of it."

In common with most apocalyptic visionaries, de Grimston saw his followers as those who would come through the cataclysm unscathed:

And by then we must be free if we are ever to be free. By then the bonds that bind us must be broken, and we must stand above the terror of the End, aloof, detached, a part of something new. For with every end there is a new beginning, and if we are not of the End then we shall be of the New Beginning.

It was another part of the Process theology that got them the Satanist label. They worshiped four gods, or four aspects of a single god. One, called Satan, was the representative of lust, violence, and excess, but also of detachment, mysticism, and asceticism. In addition to this view of Satan, there were rumors that the initiation ceremonies of the Process involved savage sex. By the 1970s, Process spokesmen denied that this was true, though they did admit that their ceremonies and philosophy had evolved and softened a great deal over the years.

When they first came to America, the Processeans paraded around in satanic-looking black robes, and were often accompanied by fierce-looking dogs. However, they soon changed their robes to a more benign navy blue. Even their dogs seemed friendlier.

The Process invited observers to their services, which were quite impressive and not at all satanic. Leaders (though not de Grimston himself) talked quite freely to reporters. But it remained a strictly hierarchical organization, and most observers felt the doctrines presented to the public, and to new converts and lower-level members, were quite different from those held by the group's inner circle. It was believed that at its core the Process possessed a secret and perhaps satanic doctrine.

In May 1974, the Process, which had always prided itself on evolving, underwent a major revolution. Robert de Grimston was thrown out, and control was apparently seized by his wife, who, according to rumor, had always been the real power in the group anyway.

The name was changed from The Process Church of the Final Judgment to the more hopeful Foundation Church of the Millennium. One group leader said, "We finally admitted that the doctrine of loving Satan never made much sense. . . . It was like deciding to have a tooth pulled. It hurt, but if we didn't do it the whole jaw might rot. It's an elegant mental construction, but it really does take a quantum leap to get from loving your enemies to loving Satan."

Most cults do not survive this sort of revolutionary change. The newly formed Foundation hung on for a while, and then, like so many other cults, just disappeared.

———

That, in brief, is the public history of Satanism in America. It is not very frightening. Aleister Crowley and Anton LaVey are nowhere near as scary as Jim Jones or David Koresh. Why then this widespread terror of a vast and powerful satanic conspiracy? We will look next at the theory of secret Satanism.

SECRET
SATANISM

Perhaps your town or neighborhood has had a "satanic scare." A cemetery might be desecrated, and satanic symbols or paraphernalia left behind. The remains of animals, apparently sacrificed as part of a satanic ritual, are found. Or, more horribly a crime—even a murder—is seen to have satanic connections. Rumors of a secret satanic cult sweep the area. The newspapers print the alarming opinions of various "experts" on Satanism. There may be lectures by some of these same experts at local schools and churches. Some local law enforcement officials may even be sent to special training seminars that teach them how to deal with the menace.

But in the end very little seems to result. The Satanists, when and if they are identified, usually turn out to be a few teenagers—the sort who are always described as "troubled." They know little or nothing of Satanism. In July 1984, there was a cemetery desecration on Long Island, New York. The vandals left behind the spray-painted inscription "SATIN LIVES." Writer Ron Rosenbaum noted, "The self-proclaimed Satanists couldn't even spell their dread Lord's name."

The great satanic conspiracy is never uncovered, and the story dies away for a time, only to surface again in some other community. Survey after survey has shown that a large percentage of the American public is deeply concerned over the existence of a vast and powerful network of murderous satanic cults—despite the fact that there is no solid evidence that such a cult network exists or ever has. What's going on?

———

For a long time the devil was not taken too seriously by most Americans. In films like *The Devil and Daniel Webster*, made in 1941 and based on an earlier story by Stephen Vincent Benét, and the 1950s Broadway musical and film *Damn Yankees*, the devil is almost a comic character. One could hardly imagine this sort of devil presiding over infant sacrifices.

Since Satanism and popular culture have always been closely linked, it is not hard to measure the change in attitudes. There was nothing amusing about the Satanism in the novel *Rosemary's Baby*, which was made into an extremely popular film in 1968. *The Exorcist*, a novel about the demonic possession of a young girl, was made into a film released in 1973. It was even more terrifying and its impact was greater because it was supposed to be based on a real case. A lot of people thought, and still think, that the film is an accurate representation of something that actually happened. *The Exorcist* was one of the most successful and widely discussed movies in the history of Holly-

———

wood. After *The Exorcist* there were many well-publicized claims of people having been "possessed" by the devil, a notion that twenty years earlier would have seemed a quaint superstition to most Americans.

And it wasn't just popular culture. In November 1972, Pope Paul VI created a worldwide sensation when in a speech he called the devil, "a living spiritual being, perverted and perverting. A terrible reality. Mysterious and frightening." Indeed, even before the Pope had spoken, a survey made by the Opinion Research Center of Chicago indicated that among Americans, belief in the reality of the devil had grown over the previous decade, while belief in God had declined. More people still believed in God than in the devil, but the gap had narrowed considerably.

Satan was no longer a joking matter.

Some, particularly fundamentalist and evangelical Christians, saw evidence of satanic influence everywhere, and it was most sinister and pervasive in those areas that influenced children and young people. Rock music, particularly that brand of rock known as heavy metal, was constantly being pointed out as evidence of Satan's plot against the young. Heavy metal bands took names like Black Sabbath and regularly used satanic symbols and lyrics. Some rock music was supposed to contain hidden satanic messages that could only be heard if the record was played backward. In reality, no evidence exists of serious satanic activity or interest among heavy metal performers. Heavy metal is a type of music that by its very nature seeks to shock and anger conventional society—most specifically parents, teachers, the clergy, and other symbols of adult authority. The satanic motif is a quick and effective way of accomplishing that end.

Another, less obvious target of the Satan hunters has been the popular role-playing game, Dungeons and Dragons. On the surface Dungeons and Dragons seems drawn from mythology and the world of J.R.R. Tolkien, rather than from anything satanic. But the talk of wizards and enchantments, plus the almost fanatical devotion the game can inspire in its enthusiasts, has been enough to set alarm bells ringing in many Christian groups. They have linked the game to teen suicide, even murder. They see involvement in the Dungeons and Dragons world as opening a door to the mind through which satanic influences may enter.

Even something as apparently benign as *The Wizard of Oz*, with its good witch and wicked witch, has been viewed with suspicion and hostility.

In the late 1960s and early 1970s, when cults became big news in America, many of the most vigorous anticult activists were fundamentalists who saw all cults, no matter what their origins or beliefs, as essentially satanic. Deprogramming of cult members, which began at that time, often resembled exorcism. And a lot of parents believed that their children who had joined cults were, in fact, "possessed." The testimony of former cult members who had been "saved" by deprogramming tended to reinforce this view.

SATANIC RITUAL ABUSE

By the 1980s a new and far more terrifying element had been added to the picture of satanic cult activity—a growing belief in the widespread ritual abuse and murder of children by once-respected professionals like day-care workers and teachers and, most frightening of all, their own parents.

This new trend began in 1980 with the publication of the book *Michelle Remembers* by a thirty-year-old Canadian named Michelle Smith and her psychiatrist Lawrence Pazder (who later became her husband). After four years of psychotherapy, Michelle suddenly began to "remember" being made to participate in the horrific ceremonies of a satanic cult when she was a child. Her mother, who had died when Michelle was fourteen, was supposed to have been a member of the cult. The ceremonies included an appearance by Satan himself, complete with horns and tail, at which he gave his "Master Plan" for the world, recited in doggerel verse. Though Michelle had been consciously aware of having an unhappy childhood, she "recovered" these deeply buried memories only in a self-induced hypnotic trance during therapeutic sessions. In what might be called her normal life, she had remembered nothing of Satanism.

Michelle Remembers was by no means the first book of its kind. Back in the 1950s, a Colorado woman who had been hypnotized "recalled" her past life in nineteenth-century Ireland. The result was a best-seller titled *The Search for Bridey Murphy*, which inspired thousands of past-life memories from other hypnotized subjects. Though not as popular as they were during the Bridey Murphy craze, past-life tales are still common today. In the 1960s a New Hampshire couple, troubled by bad dreams, went to a psychiatrist and under hypnosis recalled being kidnapped by space aliens and taken aboard a UFO. A best-seller called *Interrupted Journey* based on this account also inspired hundreds of similar tales from people who, under hypnosis, remembered their own abductions by the aliens.

While the past-life and UFO-abduction stories were generally viewed with amused tolerance by most people, tales of satanic cult activity created quite a different reaction. At about the time that *Michelle Remembers* was published, there was growing concern in America about the problem of hidden child abuse; that is, that there was a lot more child abuse going on than was generally acknowledged. Authorities, it was said, failed to believe children when they reported being abused. It was supposed that many children were afraid to report abuse or totally repressed memories of abuse out of fear. Among many religious people there was already a predisposition to believe in the possibility of widespread but carefully hidden satanic influence. Satanists, of course, were assumed to be capable of anything.

The best-known example of what could happen when these beliefs came together was the McMartin Preschool case in California. Peggy McMartin Buckey and her son, Raymond Buckey, along with five other child-care workers, were charged with molesting hundreds of children over a ten-year period. As the case grew, the accusations became more and more elaborate and exotic, including tales of satanic rituals. Michelle Smith and other "survivors" of satanic cult abuse met with children and parents in the McMartin case. Prosecutors used *Michelle Remembers* as a sort of guide to satanic abuse. None of the more sensational charges of satanic ritual abuse ever made it into court because of complete lack of evidence. The ground on which the school had stood was completely dug up by searchers looking for underground tunnels and the bones of sacrificial victims that were supposed to be there. Nothing was ever found. Yet these unsupported stories were reported in complete and gory detail in news accounts. And they were believed. Surveys showed that at the time of the trials over 95 percent of the local residents believed that the defendants were guilty.

Eventually, however, most of the charges were dropped, and others resulted either in acquittal or mistrial. It was the longest, most expensive court case in United States history. Yet even in an atmosphere of near hysteria, no one was ever found guilty of anything. But many lives were ruined, for once an accusation of child molestation is made it sticks, no matter how thin the evidence or absurd the charge seems. The McMartin case was just the first in well over one hundred similar cases in which children have made incredible accusations of abuse and satanic rituals, involving cannibalism and human sacrifice, against child-care workers or family members. In some instances defendants have been found guilty and sentenced to long prison terms.

The public appetite for tales of satanic abuse appears endless. A 1988 NBC special entitled *Devil Worship, Exposing Satan's Underground* became one of the most widely watched documentaries in TV history. It was hosted by the sensationalist journalist Geraldo Rivera, who, a day earlier, had done a show entitled "Satanic Breeders: Babies for Sacrifice." And Geraldo wasn't the only one. The talk shows were filled with people—almost all of them women—who recounted their recovered memories of being forced to take part in satanic rituals in which they saw or were forced to take part in scores of human sacrifices. A 1991 Geraldo show featured a woman who insisted that she had murdered forty children while she was in a satanic cult but had totally forgotten about what she had done until her memories were recovered in therapy.

A best-seller in Christian bookstores in 1988 was a book called *Satan's Underground*, which was supposed to be a true account of satanic ritual abuse. It was endorsed by several popular Christian authors, but was also attacked as a hoax in the Christian magazine *Cornerstone*. The attack portrayed the author of the book as mentally unstable, and a person who had a long history of making sexual accusations that were never verified. As a result of the *Cornerstone* article, the publisher eventually withdrew *Satan's Underground*, but this did not stem the tide of satanic ritual abuse stories.

Among those who style themselves experts in satanic cults, it is commonly reported that there are anywhere from 50,000 to 60,000 satanic human sacrifices in the United States every year! This is a staggering number; the total of known homicides in this very violent country is less than 25,000 a year. No corpses are ever found, the "experts" say, because Satanists generally eat their victims or possess highly sophisticated methods of disposing of the bodies. The victims are never missed because they are infants specially bred for human sacrifice, or runaways and homeless people who have no one to care about them.

Satanic cults are also supposed to be responsible for the outbreaks of cattle mutilations that seem to sweep the Western states from time to time. Most official investigations of these incidents have found that there is nothing unusual going on and that the cattle have died from natural causes. The "mutilations" are actually the work of small predators like weasels. But a book called *Cults That Kill*, by Larry Kahaner, tells the tale of a young woman who claimed to be a former member of a satanic cult that mutilated animals. Her cult, which consisted of "doctors, lawyers, veterinarians," were taught by the vets how to kill the animals and remove their blood and organs for satanic rites. But she said more:

When using the helicopter [the cult members] sometimes picked up the cow by using a homemade ... sling ... and they would move it and drop it further down from where the mutilations occurred. This would account for there not being any footprints or tire tracks. ... When using the van trucks they would also have a telescoping lift which ... was about 200 feet long mounted outside the truck and would use that to extend a man out to the cow, and he would mutilate it from a board platform on the end of the boom and he would never touch the ground. ... They sometimes do three or four cows.

Trucks with 200-foot booms and hovering helicopters should attract a good deal of attention in rural America—but when they are involved in satanic rituals they never seem to be noticed.

Belief in widespread satanic ritual abuse (often called simply SRA) has produced some strange alliances. Those who believe most deeply are fundamentalist Christians. But there is also a good deal of support for the idea among mental health professionals as well. In a two-part article called "Remembering Satan" in *The New Yorker*, author Lawrence Wright wrote:

A 1991 survey of members of the American Psychological Association found that thirty percent of the respondents had treated at least one client who claimed to have suffered from satanic ritual abuse, and ninety-three percent of those who completed a second survey believed their clients' claims to be true. Another poll addressed the opinions of social workers in California. Nearly half of those interviewed accepted the idea that S.R.A. involved a national conspiracy of multi-generational abusers and baby-killers and that many people were prominent in their communities and appeared to live completely exemplary lives. A majority of those polled believed that victims of such abuse were likely to have repressed the memories of it and that hypnosis increased the likelihood of accurately recalling what had happened.

Even stranger allies for the fundamentalists come from the ranks of committed feminists. The Los Angeles County Commission for Women formed a special task force to alert the public to the reality and dangers of satanic ritual abuse. In their 1988 report, which has been widely circulated, the task force said:

> Ritual abuse is usually carried out by members of a cult. The purpose of the ritual elements of the abuse seems threefold: (1) rituals in some groups are part of a shared belief or worship system into which the victim is being indoctrinated; (2) rituals are used to intimidate victims into silence; (3) ritual elements (e.g. devil worship, animal or human sacrifice) seem so unbelievable to those unfamiliar with these crimes that the elements detract from the credibility of the victims and make prosecution of the crimes very difficult.

In December 1992, members of the task force charged that Satanists were poisoning them and other satanic abuse survivors and their therapists "by exposing them to a toxic pesticide pumped into their offices, homes, and cars." Members of the task force said that some forty-three people were being slowly poisoned with the pesticide Diazinon, though no evidence of poisoning had been presented. The pesticide, which is used for killing ants, would not be terribly effective for poisoning people by pumping minute traces into their homes and offices.

Commenting on the charge in *The Skeptical Inquirer*, columnist Robert Sheaffer noted: "Apparently the satanic cults, which allegedly commit thousands of murders yearly without being apprehended, are nonetheless so inept as to be unable to choose an effective poison to do away with 43 of their most dangerous critics."

The January 1993 issue of *Ms.* magazine had a cover line that read "BELIEVE IT! CULT RITUAL ABUSE EXISTS." The author, who calls herself Elizabeth S. Rose, said that she was abused as a child by members of her family who were satanic cultists. She claims that she witnessed the murder of her infant sister, who was then eaten by cult members.

A whole network, indeed a virtual industry of satanic cult consultants, has grown up in response to all the interest in the subject. Aside from preachers and psychologists, there are a lot of present and former law enforcement officials, popularly called "cult cops," who travel around the country giving workshops and training seminars on what they claim is a vast and growing threat, particularly to young people.

Many of these cult cops are themselves fundamentalist Christians who insist that the only true and lasting solution to Satanism "is a personal encounter with true Christianity." Satanic cult seminars frequently cite the works of Aleister Crowley and Anton LaVey, not because they can be directly tied to the theoretical satanic conspiracy, but because they have no other prominent Satanists to quote.

As evidence of the threat, cult cops may label as satanic cases where there was no evidence of Satanism. For example, the murder of a New Jersey teenager by his friends has been called a cult killing in some seminars. Yet there was absolutely no evidence of satanic influence at all. Police who investigated the case blamed drug abuse.

Special Agent Kenneth V. Lanning, who works at the FBI behavioral sciences unit, has said that if satanic ritual murder was defined as a killing that was committed by two or more people whose primary motive was to fulfill a prescribed satanic ritual, then there is not a single documented case of satanic murder in the United States. Not one!

There have been, of course, many psychotic killers who believed, or at least said, that they were ordered to kill by Satan or demons. But other psychotic killers have said that they heard the voice of God ordering them to kill. The closest thing to a satanic ritual murder that has been documented took place in the border town of Matamoros, Mexico, in April 1989. A gang of drug smugglers had ritually killed some thirteen victims, including a University of Texas student who had been kidnapped in Brownsville, Texas. The gang seems to have mixed Afro-Caribbean religious practices with ideas that came right out of Hollywood movies on the supernatural. The case was extensively investigated, and no evidence was found that this particular group had any connection with any other cult in the United States or elsewhere.

Another case that attracted a great deal of attention was that of Paul Ingram, a police officer in Olympia, Washington, who was accused by his daughters of ritually abusing them. The girls also accused two of Ingram's friends of being part of the satanic cult. The case traumatized Olympia, but when it came to trial the two Ingram friends were acquitted for total lack of evidence. However, Ingram, who had first denied the charges, finally confessed to them. Paul Ingram was a deeply religious man who believed that Satan had the power to control people's lives and then wipe out the memories of what they had done. His confessions came after many sessions with his own minister and various self-styled cult experts and therapists. Ingram had come to believe that he had indeed been a practicing Satanist who had been made to forget years of ritual abuse of the children he always thought he had loved. He pleaded guilty but later insisted that all his recovered memories of satanic ceremonies were false. It was too late. He was not allowed to withdraw his guilty plea and was sent to jail.

Among psychologists there has been something of a backlash against the whole idea that memories of such events as witnessing or taking part in repeated ritual murders can really be repressed, and then brought back to the conscious mind years later by therapy or hypnotism. The critics point to the fact that most people who have witnessed or taken part in terrible and traumatic events remember them all too well. They also note that it is remarkably easy to plant very realistic false memories in susceptible individuals.

Richard Ofshe, a University of California psychologist and expert on cults and mind control, examined Paul Ingram, and during the course of his examination tried a little experiment. He fabricated an imaginary incident of Ingram's sexual abuse of his son and daughter. At first Ingram denied that he had ever done such a thing. Ingram was repeatedly urged to try to "remember" what had happened. After a while he produced a detailed written confession to an act of which he had never even been accused.

In 1992 a group of psychologists banded together to form the False Memory Syndrome Foundation. The purpose of the group is to combat what they see as a fast-spreading epidemic of dubious "recovered memory" therapy. This sort of therapy, say Foundation members, may be the number one mental-health crisis of the 1990s.

Lawrence Wright's detailed analysis of the Paul Ingram case concludes: "Whatever the value of repression as a scientific concept or a therapeutic tool, unquestioning belief in it has become as dangerous as the belief in witches. One idea is modern and the other an artifact of what we like to think of as a credulous age, but the consequences, depressingly, are the same."

Those who question or criticize the reality of a vast, powerful, and secret satanic cult conspiracy are accused of being naive or, worse, part of the conspiracy. If the stories of those who say they have been ritually abused are doubted, the doubters are said to be "blaming the victim." One phrase that is frequently repeated is "believe the children." For those who are deeply committed to the idea of a gigantic satanic cult conspiracy that regularly commits the most gruesome crimes as part of its rituals, an accusation is all the proof they need. To ask for more would be "revictimizing the victim," they say.

Writing in the Newsletter of the Cult Crime Impact Network, Larry Jones, a Boise, Idaho, police officer, says, "Those who deny, explain away, or cover up the obvious undeniably growing mountain of evidence often demand statistical evidence or positive linkages between . . . suspect groups. At best, this demand for positive proof of a . . . conspiracy is naive."

In response to the growing number of critics who demand evidence of cult crimes, people like Jones speak of the existence of an ever-larger conspiracy that acts to cover up the satanic crimes. Since the collapse of Communism, the satanic conspiracy has replaced the Communist conspiracy as the number one threat to America and its children in the minds of many.

THE WITCH CULTS

For many Americans the terms witchcraft and Satanism are synonymous. If a person claims to be a witch or a member of a witchcraft group, he or she by definition is a Satanist.

Not so, protest the witches. Such an identification, they say, is based on ancient prejudice and misunderstanding. In the past, these misconceptions have led to hideous persecutions during which thousands of completely innocent people were tortured, burned, and hanged. While the persecution of accused witches was never as severe in America as it was in Europe, some of the last major witchcraft trials in the Western world were those that took place in Salem, Massachusetts, in 1692. The Salem witchcraft trials—among the most famous events in American history—resulted in the death by hanging of nineteen accused witches. Another was "pressed" to death.

People think that they know what witches are, or are supposed to be, but in truth the history, and indeed the very definitions of witch and witchcraft, are extremely fuzzy. Europeans tended to label those Native Americans or Africans who practiced their traditional religions or were supposed to have magical or healing powers as "witch doctors." After the triumph of Christianity in Europe, individuals who continued to practice some of the old pagan folk rituals—particularly those involving healing or ensuring the fertility of crops and livestock—were said to be practicing "witchcraft." While such practices were officially condemned by the Church for centuries, they did not arouse great alarm or hostility.

But by the fifteenth century the beliefs and rituals of a wide variety of sects that were considered heretical, as well as many magical practices that had arisen during the Christian era, were also lumped together under the label of witchcraft, and the stage was set for the great waves of witchcraft persecution. Europe became gripped by an obsessive fear of a gigantic satanic conspiracy whose agents, the witches, engaged in human sacrifice and cannibalism and whose aim was to overthrow the Christian religion. The fear of witchcraft persisted right through the Protestant Reformation, and just about the only thing that both Catholics and Protestants agreed on was the reality of witchcraft.

By the late seventeenth century the fear had begun to die down, and the persecution tapered off and then stopped. Just a few years after the last witchcraft trials in Salem, many of those who sat in judgment of the accused witches repented, and in a statement said that they had "the guilt of innocent blood" on their hands. Rationalist thinkers of the eighteenth century

looked back on what had happened and declared that it had all been the result of medieval superstition and hysteria and that there never had been any conspiracy of witches. The term "witch hunting" came to mean persecuting people with whom one disagrees or looking for imaginary crimes and conspiracies.

The view that witchcraft was an imaginary crime became the dominant one, particularly among educated people. The witch, generally imagined as an ugly old woman wearing a black cloak and a peaked hat, became a stock character in fairy tales; she was a figure made up to frighten children, not someone who was to be taken seriously by intelligent adults.

WITCHES REEXAMINED

In the 1920s, a British scholar named Margaret Murray reexamined some of the evidence that had been produced at the European witch trials and came to a very surprising conclusion. Yes, she said, there had been real witches. In fact, there had been a large and powerful underground witch religion—a witch cult, she called it. But these witches were not the baby-killing, devil worshipers that their enemies had proclaimed them to be; rather, they were followers of an ancient and well-organized pagan religion that predated Christianity but had been forced underground by militant Christians. Among the deities worshiped by the witch religion was a horned god—hence the confusion with the Christian devil. Unlike Christianity, she said, the witch cult was a religion in which women played a significant leadership role, and that is why most of those persecuted as witches were women.

At first, Murray's theory of a witch cult got a lot of serious attention from other scholars. But in later works she went on to try to prove that well-known historical figures like Joan of Arc and many of the kings of England had really been devotees of the witch cult. At that point scholars began regarding her as a crank. But her books were still popular with the general public, particularly that segment of the public interested in the occult.

One of the legacies Professor Murray bequeathed to modern witchcraft was the coven of thirteen. She said that witches were organized into small independent groups or covens made up of thirteen individuals. Others say that she simply misinterpreted the already highly suspect evidence from the witchcraft trials.

Margaret Murray was followed by the poet and scholar Robert Graves. In his book *The White Goddess*, he held that mankind's original religion was the worship of a Mother Goddess, and that this worship was ultimately driven underground by the rise of a male-dominated Judeo-Christian tradition. Graves contended that these old religious beliefs surfaced in medieval witchcraft.

Professor Murray said that the witch cult had been completely wiped out during the witchcraft persecutions. In the 1940s, Gerald Gardner, a former British customs official in Malaya and a man of wide-ranging and often strange interests, stepped forward to disagree. Yes, he said, Professor Murray was right about the existence of an underground witch cult, but she was wrong when she said the cult had been exterminated. He claimed that he was a practicing witch and a member of an ancient coven that had carried on the traditions of what he called the "Old Religion" for many centuries.

According to Gardner, he had been contacted by a representative from this ancient group of British witches shortly before the outbreak of World War II. The witches agreed to initiate Gardner into their coven because of his interest in the occult and because some of his own ancestors had been witches. A few years later, said Gardner, his superiors gave him permission to "go public." Gardner also claimed that his coven had kept Hitler from invading England during World War II by performing a powerful magical spell, and that earlier British witches had used the same power successfully against both Napoleon and the Spanish Armada.

There has never been any independent evidence that Gardner ever was in contact with any ancient witch coven. Gardner's witchcraft—the Old Religion, the Craft, or Wicca ("the wise"), as it has been called—looks like a ragbag collection of ideas and ceremonies drawn from nineteenth- and early twentieth-century occultism. The general opinion, even among occultists sympathetic to Gardner's brand of witchcraft, is that his tale of being in contact with an ancient witch coven was a complete fabrication. It is common for occultists to claim that they are in contact with some sort of secret society that is heir to all manner of ancient wisdom.

True or not, Gardner's tale caught the public fancy. Certainly one of the reasons was that Gardner's witches were supposed to hold their ceremonies "skyclad," or in the nude. This conjured up images of sexual orgies. But that, according to Gardner's followers, is a false idea. Raymond Buckland, who was Gardner's chief American disciple, wrote:

> The reasons for nudity are several, but sex does not enter into it. Firstly the nakedness is a sign of freedom; of a casting off of worldly things. The Ceremony of Drawing Down the Moon contains some words said by the High Priestess as the Goddess: ". . . and as a sign that ye be free ye shall be naked in your rites. . . ." But the most important reason for being skyclad is the belief in a power which comes from the human body.

Photos of nude witches performing their ceremonies began appearing in the more daring magazines of the 1950s. Today virtually every book on witchcraft or the occult contains one or more pictures of nude witches performing their ceremonies.

GERALD B. GARDNER, THE SELF-PROCLAIMED SPOKESPERSON FOR AN ANCIENT WITCH COVEN.

About the nude rites, Gardner wrote in 1955, "In these days of nudist clubs is that so very terrible?" The witchcraft rites in the Gardnerian tradition do not sound shocking; they sound downright dull. But there were rumors that Gardner was less than perfectly honest about what went on, and that both sex and ritual flagellation were also involved in his witchcraft ceremonies. But compared with today's rumors of mass infant sacrifice, even that doesn't sound very shocking.

The witchcraft rituals of Gardner and his followers use the magic circles, the swords, the chants, and other elements drawn from what is called ceremonial magic. It is a collection of magical lore—some ancient, some not so ancient—that became very popular in Britain in the late nineteenth and early twentieth centuries.

Gardner's witchcraft also incorporated elements from many other occult sources. In addition, it carried with it an aura of ancient British or Celtic romanticism, the sort of atmosphere that was popular in the works of Sir Walter Scott. According to one observer of the occult scene, Gardner "worked taking material from any source that didn't run too fast to get away."

Gerald Gardner himself never had a large personal following, nor did he seem to seek one. But his tale of an ancient witch religion existing into modern times inspired all sorts of people, first in Britain and then in the United States, to "come out of the closet" and declare that they, too, were witches. In addition to those who said, like Gardner, that they were hereditary witches, there were plenty who lined up to be initiated into a coven. When Gardner first announced that he was a witch, he said sadly that witchcraft was "a dying cult," and one of the reasons that he went public was that he wanted authentic information about the Old Religion passed on to the general public before it was lost entirely. Before his own death in 1964, however, Gardner was forced to admit that the cult wasn't dying after all, for so many witches had gone public and so many new covens were being formed. Many of these new witchcraft groups offered alternatives to pure Gardnerian witchcraft, and the Old Religion, like many newer ones, was split into rival movements and sects.

At first Gardner and his followers stirred up a great deal of anger among those people, especially religious fundamentalists, for whom the very word "witch" is a red flag. But the British public has a high tolerance for eccentricity, if it is specifically British. For many years the British have revered a group calling itself the Ancient Order of Druids. These Druids parade around in long white robes, and sometimes wear false beards. They claim to be the direct descendants of the Druids who were priests of the ancient Britons, though there is not a shred of evidence to support such a claim. The Druids held a well-publicized ceremony every year at Stonehenge on the day of the summer solstice. That practice ended in 1985 because spectators became too rowdy. Gardnerian witches attained almost that degree of respectability, and Gardner himself was actually invited to Buckingham Palace for an audience with the Queen.

In the United States, where the fires of religious fundamentalism burn more brightly, witchcraft has never become that respectable, though it is recognized as a genuine religion for tax purposes by the Internal Revenue Service. In most large cities people can proclaim themselves to be witches without getting into any trouble. In a few places like San Francisco, California, and Salem, Massachusetts (which now uses its tragic history of witchcraft hysteria as a tourist attraction), there are official or semi-official witches who preside at Halloween parades and give lots of interviews late in October. In rural or less sophisticated parts of the country, people who say they are witches have been harassed and sometimes driven from their homes.

In the late 1960s and early 1970s, there was a major upsurge of interest in witchcraft—or neo-Paganism, as it came to be called. There were a number of reasons for this. Like the Old Religion, filled with images of sacred groves, the rhythm of the seasons, and invocation of natural forces, it seemed to harmonize with a growing interest in ecology.

Witchcraft was also a religion in which women

held an equal, if not dominant position, and that was attractive to some in the growing women's movement. One of the early, and highly visible, radical feminist groups was called WITCH—Women's International Terrorist Corps from Hell. Carrying brooms and wearing black robes and peaked hats, the members of WITCH often appeared at women's rights demonstrations. WITCH was part put-on, part guerrilla theater, and part serious. The fact that most of those who were persecuted during the witchcraft hysteria were women led to a serious study of historical witchcraft by feminist scholars and writers. Indeed, the growing public popularity of witchcraft led to an general increase of historical scholarship in the subject.

In 1992, Pat Robertson, a leader in the religious right, accused feminists of advocating witchcraft. This statement, made in a fund-raising letter, attracted a great deal of hostile attention, and Robertson tried to distance himself from it, but he never disavowed it, and the charge is still widely believed in the ranks of the religious right.

The absence of a rigid morality, and willingness to include all sorts of different traditions into witchcraft, appealed to those who in the 1960s and 1970s believed that it was the dawning of the Age of Aquarius.

The lack of a consistent philosophy didn't bother Gardner much, nor did it bother others who claimed to be witches. They saw many forces at work in the universe, and believed that knowledge and power can come from many sources. Those in the Judeo-Christian tradition, the witches say, suffer from a sort of tunnel vision in which they see only one source for truth and power. Thus the charge that modern witches are inconsistent really misses the point, for in their view there is no need for consistency. In the past, pagans freely accepted one another's gods and rituals without being hypocritical.

The more closely one looked at modern witchcraft, the more difficult it became to insist that it was an ancient belief handed down secretly from generation to generation for thousands of years. P. E. I. Bonewits, who is both an occultist and historian of the occult has said: "Never at any time until the persecution of the mid-1400s to the mid-1700s were witches considered by anyone (priest, magician, wizard or peasant) to be representatives of an underground religious movement."

He went on to say, "I am not attacking the religious or mystical significance of witchcraft. It brings much comfort and happiness to its members. I just wish that it would accept the fact that it is a 20th century reconstruction of elements from various prehistoric fertility religions, and stop trying to be something it is not."

Most witches would argue with such a view, but in their generally easygoing manner they would agree that a tradition like theirs did not have to be ancient or "pure" in order to be effective. In short, "If it's all made up, so what. It works for me."

For a while the movement seemed to flourish with an estimated forty to fifty thousand practicing witches in the United States alone, though the number is quite impossible to verify. But witchcraft was never really organized, and the witch groups or covens were not structured in a way that encouraged the emergence of the sort of charismatic and all-powerful leader that is necessary for the development of what can properly be called a cult. A libertarian freedom of thought and action was basic to witchcraft groups. In fact, hostility toward modern witchcraft actually seemed to decline in the United States during the 1980s. When dangerous cults were listed, witch and pagan groups were rarely mentioned. The witches had agitated, with considerable success, to have their beliefs and practices separated from those of Satanists, with whom they had been so often linked. Witches always stressed that they practiced "white magic," that is, benign or helpful magic, rather than "black magic," or magic aimed at producing evil. Indeed one of the tenets of many witch groups is that if you do an evil it will rebound against you—if not in this life, then in the next. The country's best-known Satanist, Anton LaVey, openly sneered at what he called "tea shoppe witches."

By the 1990s, however, the popularity of modern witchcraft seemed to be fading. Since it was never possible to determine how many people were actually committed to witchcraft, it is of course impossible to know how far their numbers have fallen. But there has certainly been a sharp drop in publicity, and witchcraft, though it was supposed to be a secretive practice, thrived on publicity. Indeed there are those who insist that modern witchcraft was never really a serious belief at all, but that it was mainly show business; publicity for individuals who were supporting themselves with lecture fees, or by writing books and conducting courses on "real" witchcraft; or simply for people who liked to get on television and generally be noticed. There is probably a good deal of truth in such a charge.

Religious groups that have stepped up their denunciations of all occult groups and practices have once again begun to energetically denounce witchcraft—but there now is very little left to denounce. Witchcraft seems to have been absorbed into that large and amorphous body of beliefs and practices known as New Age Religion.

God, Mantras, and the Hollow Earth

The United States has been the home of an incredible variety of cults, with a bewildering range of beliefs and lifestyles. They were not all as grim and terrible as the Peoples Temple or the Branch Davidians. Here are brief accounts of just a few that will provide a hint of the diversity.

FATHER DIVINE

Many cult leaders have declared themselves to be divinely inspired messengers of God, even messiahs, but relatively few have said flatly that they are God Himself. The most flamboyant of those who have was the man who called himself Father Divine.

He was born George Barker around 1880, the son of former slaves on a rice plantation in South Carolina. He spent his apprenticeship with a variety of black evangelists, and then in 1930 was "reborn" as God, or Father Divine.

He was a short, rather rotund man, not physically imposing at all, but he possessed enormous charisma. His flock grew during the Great Depression, and at its height may have numbered over 200,000. There were about 160 of the group's Peace Missions scattered throughout the country. The vast majority of Father Divine's followers were black, but he also attracted a modest following among whites, particularly among white women. This was a time in the history of America when a black man could be lynched for simply talking to a white woman.

There are many stories told about Father Divine. The most persistent is that when his movement was just getting started, he moved his mission into the white community of Sayville, Long Island. He was harassed by local authorities and finally hauled into court. The judge fined him $500 and sentenced him to a year in jail. Three days later the judge suddenly dropped dead.

When asked about what happened, Father Divine is said to have replied, "I hated to do it."

Followers of Father Divine were urged to be scrupulously honest. "You're either honest or dishonest," he said. They were told to work hard, and not accept government relief. Peace Missions helped people get jobs, and the group started laundries and other small businesses to help members. There was to be no alcohol, no tobacco, and no sex—not even between married couples. But there was food. The Peace Missions were famous for serving enormous twenty-course meals.

A lot of outsiders saw Father Divine as a hypocrite and racketeer. While his followers were generally poor, Father Divine lived like a king. He drove around in an

FATHER DIVINE, ENJOYING ONE OF THE SUMPTUOUS SOCIAL
CELEBRATIONS FOR WHICH HE WAS SO WELL KNOWN.

enormous, specially-built limousine, the "Throne Car." He also surrounded himself with a bevy of young women—his "angels," he called them. Father Divine always claimed that all his relationships with women were "spiritual," but cult defectors told a different story.

Father Divine promised his followers that they would not die. So every death in the group, or even an illness, was looked upon as evidence of sin. However, when it came Father's time to die, that could not be so easily explained. He is said to have announced from his deathbed that he was not really dying. "I'm just dematerializing. If it takes a millennium, I'll be repersonified in another body. I shall be back."

During his long career Father Divine was both worshiped and hated. He was an object of curiosity and the butt of a lot of jokes. There can be no doubt that he was a fraud. He lived in great luxury off the income provided by his followers. But he gave a lot of people a sense of order, dignity, and purpose. He gave people jobs at a time there were few jobs for them, and he gave them food when food was hard to come by. Most of those who had a brush with Father's Peace Missions remember them, and him, with affection.

THE SULLIVANIANS

The stereotype of a cult member is a young person, often poorly educated, living in an isolated community presided over by a wild-eyed fanatic who says he is getting messages from God. The well-educated professionals who were living communally in two very nice buildings in Manhattan do not fit the popular image; nonetheless, they were cult members.

The Sullivanians were therapists, patients, and their families associated with the Sullivan Institute for Research in Psychoanalysis. The group was named after Harry Stack Sullivan, a well-known psychiatrist who died in 1949. The leader of the group, Saul Newton, had been a student of Sullivan's and admired him greatly. People who came to one of the Sullivanian therapists for help with psychological problems were gradually drawn into the community.

According to defectors from the group, Newton and a small circle of close associates regulated virtually every aspect of group life. They planned love affairs, arranged marriages and divorces, decided whether or not a couple could have a child, or if they had one, how much time they could spend with the child. People inside the cult were forbidden to have close relationships with their families outside the cult. One woman reported that after her son became involved with the group, he returned a Christmas present she sent him and threatened to call a lawyer if she ever sent him another one. Newton believed that it was his mission to create a better world, and one way to do that was to keep people from becoming "too focused" on one another.

Decisions about individual behavior were passed on to the therapist who was dealing with that individual. Disobeying the directives could result in heavy fines, sometimes amounting to thousands of dollars.

Sullivanian therapy itself was extremely expensive, and placed great financial burdens even on the affluent patients. The therapists, however, prospered, sometimes earning as much as $100,000 a year. In addition to a couple of apartment buildings, the group also owned other valuable real estate in Greenwich Village and upstate New York. At its peak during the 1970s the Sullivanian cult had some 400 members.

In addition to his bizarre theories of personal behavior, Newton's other ideas and fears were imposed on the community. When there was a serious nuclear reactor accident at Three Mile Island in Pennsylvania in 1979, Newton panicked and he and many of the community members fled to Florida. They returned about a week later equipped with Geiger counters for taking radiation levels, and they started buying special vehicles which they hoped would help them flee the next nuclear emergency.

AIDS created such fear that community members were not allowed to eat in restaurants within a fifty-mile (80-kilometer) radius of New York City. When they walked their dogs on the city streets they had to wash the animals' paws before bringing them back into the building, to prevent them from tracking in the AIDS virus.

The fears, even some of the theories of human behavior, were common enough, but under the direction of an autocrat whose decisions could not be questioned, and in the hothouse atmosphere of a closed community, people's lives were being seriously warped.

By the 1980s the community had begun to unravel. Defectors and relatives of those who were still members formed an organization called PACT, People Against Cult Therapy. They went to the media, and sensational stories about the group, which had looked so respectable to outsiders, began to appear. Newton called his opponents "liars and crooks," but in general he tried to hide from the press. Saul Newton finally died in 1991. At this writing, the community, now much reduced in size, still hangs on. But its days are clearly numbered.

TRANSCENDENTAL MEDITATION

For well over a century a variety of gurus, or teachers, from India have come to the West. Some have attracted good-sized followings, but none has had the impact of the Maharishi Mahesh Yogi. In the 1950s this onetime hermit decided that his mission was the spiritual regeneration of all mankind.

In order to reach Westerners, he refined and simplified some ancient Indian meditation practices into a technique called Transcendental Meditation, or TM. It could be taught quickly and simply in a technological society where everyone was always in a hurry.

The Maharishi's movement got a tremendous boost when he picked up some celebrity followers. The first were the Beatles, particularly George Harrison. The singing group had moved from psychedelic drugs to meditation. Their infatuation with the Maharishi, however, did not last long. One member of the group was quite bitter about it, describing the whole experience as a "bad trip." Another famous convert was the actress Mia Farrow.

The Maharishi's popularity went into decline after the Beatles dropped him, but in 1970 he got a huge boost from a most unexpected source—science. A study published in the prestigious journal *Science*, concluded that Transcendental Meditation actually produced measurable changes in body functions. The

THE MAHARISHI, WHOSE TRANSCENDENTAL MEDITATION TECHNIQUES
ENJOYED WIDESPREAD POPULARITY DURING THE 1960s AND 1970s.

meditator could attain a state of deep and healthful relaxation.

The TM boom was on, and it was promoted as a panacea for lowering blood pressure, making people more organized and creative, kicking a drug habit, giving up smoking, and lots of other things. Hundreds of thousands signed up for the basic TM course, which took only a few hours, and cost a mere $100. During the course the student was given a "mantra," a word on which he or she was to concentrate during meditation. Each meditator was to be given a personal mantra in the ancient Indian language of Sanskrit. It turned out that there were really only about thirty mantras that were given out at random, but they were supposed to be kept absolutely secret, so people thought that they had their own special magic words.

Learning the TM technique was only the first step. It was the Maharishi's aim to produce what he called "absolute bliss consciousness." This, he said, would not only make everyone happier but, if widely practiced, would produce universal world peace. After taking the initial course the student could take more and more advanced instruction, and finally become a full-time follower of the Maharishi. At this point one became a cult member.

But the bloom soon faded from the TM rose. One of the scientists who did the study of TM wrote his own book in which he showed how a person didn't need a TM course with its mystic trappings. He claimed that the very same effects could be attained without a secret mantra—all the meditator had to do was repeat any simple word—like "one," for example. But more significantly, meditation failed to produce all the wonderful effects that had been promised. It was like a crash diet—for a while it seemed to reduce anxiety, but it was tough to stick to, and soon the anxiety returned.

The Maharishi then announced that he could teach his more advanced students to do something truly remarkable—they could learn to levitate, to defy gravity and raise themselves off the ground. There was an immediate clamor by the press for a demonstration of this marvel. For months devotees resisted, but finally the demonstration was held. What the Maharishi's followers had been taught to do is hop while sitting in the cross-legged "lotus" position. That is an impressive acrobatic feat—but it is not levitation. Since that time the Maharishi's movement has been in severe decline in the West, but it is still quite wealthy and influential in some Third World nations.

KORESHANITY

The name Koresh, Hebrew for Cyrus, that the Branch Davidian cult leader chose for himself, brings to mind another, earlier, American cult leader who called himself Koresh. In the late nineteenth century, Cyrus Reed Teed, an herbalist in Utica, New York, had a revelation. He said that the earth was hollow, and that we are living on the inside!

Many of Teed's methods of accounting for observable phenomena in terms of the hollow earth were really quite ingenious. The sun was at the center of Teed's hollow earth, and it was half light and half dark. It was the rotation of this two-sided central sun that caused the illusion that the sun rises and sets. The moon, planets, and stars were not distant objects but merely reflections of light. The reason we couldn't see across to the other side of the earth was that the atmosphere was too dense. Some of Teed's other explanations, however, were utterly incomprehensible.

Teed also decided that he was the new Messiah and adopted the name Koresh. He called his religion Koreshanity, and the hollow earth was a basic article of faith. He wrote, "To know of the earth's concavity is to know God. While to believe in the earth's convexity is to deny Him and all His works. All that is opposed to Koreshanity is antichrist."

Astonishingly, Teed managed to gather several hundred followers, partly because he was a spellbinding orator and partly because his hollow earth had a certain appeal. It made the universe smaller, more manageable, more comfortable. The earth was no longer an insignificant bit of rock orbiting an obscure star; it was the whole universe!

Koresh moved his followers to a "New Jerusalem" in Florida, and before his death in 1908 he said that he would rise from the dead. Followers kept watch over the body for two days, but in the Florida heat it quickly showed signs of decay, and health officials ordered that the Messiah of the Hollow Earth be buried. The cult lingered on and continued to make a few converts. As late as 1961, there were still thirty surviving members. The 300-acre (120-hectare) tract of land that it owned was turned over to the state of Florida for a Koreshan State Historic Park. The last Koreshanity adherent, who died in 1983, was a guide for the park.

THE MOONIES

No contemporary cult has used money and political power quite as effectively as the Unification Church, better known as the Moonies, after its founder and leader, the Korean prophet Reverend Sun Myung Moon. Moon has often been described as an evangelist, which makes him sound like a Christian preacher. He had been a Presbyterian, and some of his ideas have a Christian sound to them, but he is no Christian. Moon says that when he was seventeen he began receiving revelations from God that laid bare the "true meaning" of God's "coded message" in the Bible. Through these revelations he developed a new body of knowledge called the Divine Principles. Though Moon has not actually come out and said that he is the new Messiah, he has also very coyly refused to deny that he is.

Moon began gathering followers in Seoul, the capital of South Korea, shortly after the end of the Korean War. His mission to the United States started in earnest in 1972. In public, he tried to portray himself as a fairly orthodox Christian. But he had a weakness for staging strange spectaculars, like mass public weddings of his followers—for which Moon himself had arranged all the marriages. As the media began to probe more deeply into the Unification Church, it became clear that this was not just another Christian sect.

Despite an enormous amount of publicity, however, the Moonies were never really all that successful in winning converts in the United States. There were some, but most of those who showed up at Moon's mass rallies or peddled peanuts and dried flowers on the street to raise money for his church were Korean, Chinese, or European.

What sets the Unification Church apart from other cults of a similar nature is the enormous amount of money the group has. The source of the funds has always been something of a mystery. The money to rent

THE REVEREND SUN MYUNG MOON SPRINKLES HOLY
WATER OVER THE TWO THOUSAND COUPLES BEING UNITED
IN A MASS MARRIAGE CEREMONY AT
MADISON SQUARE GARDEN IN NEW YORK CITY.

Madison Square Garden or buy a huge estate in Tarry-town, New York, did not come from the sales of pea-nuts and dried flowers. Back in Korea, Moon's movement had originally been persecuted. But Moon made an alliance with South Korean President Chung Hee Park. Businesses owned by Moon, where followers worked long hours for no pay, were given special ad-vantages; in return, Moon supported Park.

In America, Moon showed he knew how to play the political game. He became a leading supporter of President Richard Nixon. As the Nixon presidency was coming apart during the Watergate crisis, Moon spon-sored full-page ads in major newspapers proclaiming "GOD LOVES NIXON." His followers held a series of dem-onstrations in Washington, D.C., in which they prayed for Nixon. Moon himself was invited to the White House to be photographed beside the beleaguered president.

Moon money has backed a large number of con-ferences of scholars and politicians, in what is clearly an effort to buy access and influence. The Unification Church also owns the *Washington Times*, a right-wing newspaper in the nation's capital.

It was money, however that finally got Moon into real trouble. He was convicted on a variety of tax charges and spent over a year in jail. Full-page ads proclaimed that Reverend Moon was the victim of "religious persecution." But Moon survived his im-prisonment, and so did his organization. Smiling and confident, he once again proclaimed his love for America.

Despite his conviction, his singular lack of suc-cess in gaining American converts, and his inability to speak English, Reverend Moon seems to have set up his permanent home in the United States. He is less flamboyant than he was before his jail term; there have been no mass rallies or mass weddings recently. But as long as his finances remain secure, the Unification Church will probably continue until his death.

Then there will be a crisis. One of Moon's beliefs is that Jesus was a failed Messiah because he was not supposed to die. What will happen to his followers when Moon dies?

INSIDE A CULT

In early September 1993, another horrifying cult story hit the headlines and all the network news programs. Even the normally sedate *New York Times* seemed swept up in the sensational nature of the account. A four-column headline read: "ARGENTINES SAY A SEX CULT ENSLAVED 268 CHILDREN."

The story went on to describe how 180 Argentine policemen raided the Buenos Aires headquarters of a cult called the Family, which had been under investigation for over a year. As many as sixty United States citizens were among the children and adults taken into custody. The U.S. Embassy had provided documents about three American children who supposedly were being held against their will. Since the destruction of the Branch Davidian cult, U.S. government officials have been much more active in monitoring the activities of cults.

The story continued, "For several years, the Argentine police have watched the mysterious activities of the Family as its members bought homes in the suburbs of Buenos Aires, sold posters and videotapes in the street and touched off rumors about prostitution, sex involving children and drugs."

Television news shows featured heavily censored clips from what were alleged to be these "sex videotapes."

The police found 268 children living in deplorable conditions, many underfed and poorly clothed. They also found literature promoting sex between adults and children.

In the previous year there had been similar raids against branches of the cult in Australia, France, and Spain. The group had also been expelled from China and Egypt.

According to the *Times* story, "Known in Argentina as the Family or Family of Love, the group originated with the Children of God, which emerged from the 1960s hippie movement in Huntington Beach, California."

For me, that started a lot of bells ringing. Back in the early 1970s, the Children of God (or COG) was far and away the most notorious cult in America. The whole idea of deprogramming was started by parents who were trying to get their own children out of the Children of God.

At that time there were some three thousand members of the Children of God scattered in fifty or sixty colonies (they disliked the word communes) throughout the United States. The colonies changed location frequently, often one jump ahead of the law or of angry parents who were trying forcibly to take their children back.

In 1972 one of these colonies set up quite near where I was living. Over a period of a few months, until the colony moved on, I had a chance to visit with them frequently. It would be an exaggeration to say that I got to know them well. The COG leaders were much too guarded and secretive, and behind a facade of open friendliness I knew they were trying to manipulate me. But I did get a chance to observe the workings of this colony over an extended period, and was able to learn a good deal about them, perhaps more than they wanted me to know.

The Children of God was the creation of a one-time traveling evangelist named David Berg. Berg's mother, Virginia Brandt Berg, had also been an evangelist and faith healer. In the 1940s, Berg and his family moved to California, where he worked as a sort of public relations man for radio evangelist Fred Jordan.

Berg's big chance came in 1967, when he became director of "Teen Challenge," a Christian coffeehouse in Huntington Beach, California. It was the time of the hippies, the flower children, and the drug culture. A lot of churches had opened coffeehouses in an attempt to lure disaffected teens back into the fold. But Berg was not content merely to get young people off drugs and into church and straight society in general. He wanted "one hundred percent discipleship." That meant cutting all ties with home, family, church, and established society; living communally; and spending all of one's time spreading Berg's version of Christianity.

Like that of so many other cult leaders, David Berg's vision was an apocalyptic one. He expected great catastrophes, and the end of the world. In 1968, California was swept with "earthquake fever," a belief that as a result of a great earthquake a large portion of the state was simply going to drop into the sea. This

fear was fed by occult groups and also by Christian fundamentalists, who looked upon California as a new Sodom that deserved to be destroyed for its wickedness. Caught up in the fervor, Berg loaded his followers, then numbering about fifty, into some old school buses, and led them out of the doomed land.

Berg and his followers spent about eight months wandering through the Southwest, sleeping in buses and depending on charity for food. Often there wasn't enough, and the COG later compared this period of wandering with the time that the biblical children of Israel spent wandering in the wilderness. It also set a pattern for a nomadic existence that remains to this day. Berg's followers began referring to him as Moses, or Moses David.

Despite the hardships, the group—first called Teens for Christ, then Revolutionaries for Jesus, and finally the Children of God—began picking up new members. They were extremely aggressive in their proselytizing, and they began to attract media attention. The COG members were the models for what came to be called the Jesus People or Jesus Freaks. They would often show up at rock concerts or amusement parks, anyplace where young people were likely to gather.

To say that the COG became controversial would be to describe its position in the mildest possible terms. They were accused of being everything from agents of the devil to confidence tricksters. The most common charge was that they were hypocrites who

THE CHILDREN OF GOD, POPULAR IN THE 1970s, REEMERGED IN THE 1990s WITH ACCUSATIONS OF CHILD ABUSE IN ARGENTINA.

talked of love but preached hate, and who posed as good Bible-believing Christians but lived in a way that most fundamentalists would find abhorrent and ungodly. The COG were accused of getting money under false pretenses and lying about the group's lives and goals.

Many of the charges were absolutely true, but to simply label the COG hypocrites is to misunderstand them and miss the real depth of their belief. If one has to pin a label on them, "antinomian" would probably fit best. It is not a term frequently used today. The word has been applied to Christian sects of the past in which members believed that because they were true Christians, the grace of God released them from the necessity for obeying traditional political or moral laws. Thus, it is possible to lie or cheat the people of "the World," for the world is irredeemably evil, and still not be a liar or cheat in the eyes of God. Indeed it is considered necessary to use the World's worst weapons against it to protect God's chosen but persecuted few. The COG used the biblical phrase "spoiling Egypt" or the more modern one, "ripping off the System."

To the outsider there may seem little real difference between this sort of antinomianism and hypocrisy, or plain lying. But to the believer the difference is crucial. The Children of God members were not plain religious racketeers or self-deluded fools.

Despite California's failure to fall into the sea in 1968, the COG continued to search for signs of the approaching apocalypse. In 1973 a newly discovered comet called Kohoutek was supposed to pass close to Earth around Christmas time. Some astronomers predicted it would be the brightest comet of the century.

Berg dubbed it the Christmas Monster, and members of the Children of God, dressed in long homespun robes and carrying long wooden staves, made a highly theatrical appearance in front of the United Nations building with signs warning of the approaching end. In one of his many writings on the subject of the comet, Berg said, "*You* in the U.S. have only until *January* [1974] to get *out* of the states before some kind of disaster, destruction or judgment of God is to fall because of America's wickedness. . . . *Now* is the *time*! It's *later* than you *think*! *Hallelujah*! The *End* is near!"

As it turned out, Kohoutek was a fizzle for everyone but professional astronomers. It was virtually invisible to the naked eye, and the time passed with no more than the usual disasters. But the Children of God people were undismayed. They found plenty of signs of the coming end.

Like many others who came from a fundamentalist background, David Berg has looked to political events in the Middle East, where the final battle between God and Satan is to be fought, for signs of the approaching end. In 1973 he predicted the destruction of Israel and of America. He revived the old charge that Jewish bankers are creating economic chaos throughout the world. But to the charge that he is anti-Semitic, Berg has responded that he is Jewish. He had also written many angry diatribes against Christians.

The COG had a brief and bizarre flirtation with Libya's dictator Muammar al-Qaddafi. Berg praised Qaddafi as something just short of a new Messiah. And Qaddafi, who at that time rarely saw Westerners, entertained two of Berg's children in his tent, and apparently even wrote a song for them. Berg may have viewed the Libyan dictator as a possible patron, as Qaddafi had a reputation for funneling money to dissident groups in the West. There was a flurry of publicity, but apparently nothing of substance resulted.

I was aware of most of this when I dropped in, unannounced, at a COG colony housed in a collection of old summer cottages in Sullivan County, in upstate New York. I also knew the stories of how COG members were supposed to be little more than brainwashed zombies kept under guard, drugged and starved to keep them from escaping.

Contrary to my expectations, or perhaps my fears, I was greeted with great friendliness by the colony leaders, particularly after they found out I was a writer. I was allowed to go anywhere I wished, "Just so you can see we don't have anyone chained in the cellar," one of the COG leaders joked. The accommodations were fairly primitive, and the food ran heavily to cheap fare like hot dogs and beans. But it would have been familiar to anyone who had ever been to summer camp. I saw no sign of drugs of any sort.

There were no fences, and the colony was located only a mile or so from a small city and a police station. Anyone could have walked out of the place and gone to the police.

The new members—babes, as they were called— were quite bright-eyed and unzombielike. They tended to answer most questions with a stream of stock biblical quotations, which were not always accurate. They didn't seem much different from enthusiastic if poorly informed young converts to many other religions or causes.

But things were not as free and easy as they appeared on the surface. The babes were always accompanied or closely watched by one of the elders or more senior members. The babes were mostly in their late teens; the elders were not much older, mostly in their mid- to late twenties. It would not have been easy for one of the babes to walk away unobserved. When I talked to one of the newer members, an elder was always close by to hear what was being said. If confused, the babe would look to the elder for an answer. That happened frequently.

The leaders of the community were quite candid when talking about some subjects. When I asked about the group's doctrine of "one hundred percent tithing," the response was, "Some churches tithe their members ten per cent. We take it all." How about "brainwashing?" "Sure we brainwash 'em. We clean their brains."

The leaders also spoke quite freely of how they kept angry relatives from locating young people who had joined the cult. Upon entering, everyone was given a new biblical name. So if they were asked if Joe Smith were part of the group the answer would be no. Joe Smith no longer existed; he was now Jethro. Members were constantly shifted from one colony to another, and the colonies themselves were always on the move. They were hard to pin down and hard to follow.

The COG had a slogan that usually brought people up short: "I am a toilet." When I asked what that meant, I was told that they saw themselves as a place where the human waste products from modern society could be collected and "recycled." "Out of the tank of every toilet comes God's fresh, clean water to wash away man's defilement!" This mission to collect and save the lowest of the low was hardly a new one among Christians. But the way of expressing it was offered as both a shock and a challenge.

There were some things the COG would not talk about. One was the whereabouts of David Berg. There was no question he was the absolute leader of the group; indeed his family was quite seriously called the Royal Family. But he had not been seen in public for over a year, and there were rumors he was living in England. The babes had never seen him, and the elders either didn't know where he was or wouldn't say.

They were even more unwilling to talk about sex in the group. COG leaders tried to convey the impression that traditional monogamous marriage was the norm. But it didn't take much probing to find out that this was not the case. Marriages were arranged by the group's leaders. Couples were often split up and children were rarely raised by their biological parents.

Berg controlled his far-flung group by issuing a constant flow of letters and directives called the Mo letters. Some of these were public, others private—for the eyes of the leaders only. But someone, probably a defecting member, stole some of the private letters, and they indicated that Berg and upper-level COG leaders were allowed numerous sexual partners, just like the Hebrew patriarchs. It isn't hard to use the Bible to justify polygamy. That's what Berg seemed to be doing. No one would give me a straight answer when I repeatedly asked if that was what David Berg meant.

Unlike many religious groups, the COG did not regard sex as a necessary evil. To them it was a positive joy. They were also very interested in procreation. Berg wrote to his followers: "Be fruitful and multiply—that's one of the first principles of this outfit in more ways than one. We believe in multiplication—that's part of the game—in more ways than one!"

Most of the women in the colony I visited were either pregnant or caring for infants. They were opposed to abortion, birth control, and having children in hospitals. Women gave birth to their children in the colony without medical aid and with the members of the group gathered around singing and praying.

I didn't meet a single woman in the group who held a leadership position, and I gathered that, aside from Berg's immediate family, there were none. Overall, the COG women seemed to be in a very subordinate, even downtrodden, position. They told me that this was the status that the Bible said they should have.

There were even more troubling rumors about the sexual practices of the cult. It was said that some COG women used sex to attract new converts. There was talk of the women actually being used as prostitutes to get money for the group. There was even a story that an attractive young woman who was a member of the Children of God had become the mistress of a U.S. congressman in order to gain some influence.

While the COG leaders I talked to did not confirm these stories, they did not absolutely deny them either. They talked of themselves as being "fishers of men," that is, catching new converts. Berg wrote of "flirty fishing"—as if the women were being used as bait. It is important to know that most of the COG members at that time were street kids, runaways and broken products of the drug scene. Many of the women I talked to told me that they had been prostitutes before being saved.

The leaders, however, seemed to have come from more stable religious backgrounds. They said that they had become disgusted with what they regarded as the hypocrisy of conventional churches. Even before joining the group they were well versed in apocalyptic lore and biblical literalism.

Other cults have been accused of practically working their members to death. But the COG members, as I observed them, didn't seem to work very hard at all. They kept their housing reasonably clean, repaired their vehicles, took care of their children, cooked meals, and spent an awful lot of time attending long and extremely boring Bible classes. There was also a lot of singing and Hallelujah shouting. The group's main work was gaining new converts, and this they did with great vigor. Every weekend they would get into their buses and go to places where teenagers gathered.

Though the Children of God lived simply and cheaply, it still cost money to rent places to live, buy and maintain second-hand vehicles, and feed seventy or eighty people. It was never clear to me where the money was coming from. One obvious source was new converts—upon joining the COG new members turned over everything they had and everything they could get from their parents or other relatives. One of the charges leveled against the group was that they made members break with their families, yet they continued to harass the families for donations. But they had few wealthy converts. They also said they did a lot of begging—going around to supermarkets and asking for day-old bread or dented cans of food. Perhaps significantly, those who did such foraging were called "procurers." Still there didn't seem to be enough new members or day-old bread to keep the whole operation running, and the sources of funds remained a mystery.

Overall, I got the feeling that what held this group together was not brainwashing, hypnotism, or fences. It wasn't even obedience to what they believed to be God's word, or a desire to survive the coming apocalypse. Most of these cult members had been badly treated by life. The leaders quite accurately described them as society's walking wounded. The Children of God gave them a strong sense of community and family, something they had never had before. A member was never lonely, or even alone. They didn't have to decide what to do next, or what to think. They had become a band of brothers and sisters, despised by the rest of the world, but possessing a knowledge and a state of grace that made them better than the rest of the world. Their hatred for the world, or "the System," was barely concealed behind the smiles and professions of Christian love for everyone.

The Children of God colony that I spent time with lasted only a few months—that was standard. Their neighbors, and local officials, were giving them a hard time about building codes and sanitary violations. But the COG leaders told me that they were not only getting ready to leave the area but to leave the country. There was too much hostility nationwide, and it was harder and harder to get new converts. Besides, they said, America was about to be destroyed anyway. They had glowing reports and pictures and videotapes of happy Children of God colonies being set up in South America and Europe. The COG were big on electronic gadgets. And they always took time out from what they were doing to watch the six o'clock news on television. It was almost as if they expected to see the end of the world announced on the evening news.

When they moved out they left behind two banners with ominous biblical quotations. One read:

> If they receive you not, depart and say: Even the very dust of your city which cleaveth on us, we do wipe off against you. Verily I say

unto you it shall be more tolerable for the
land of Sodom and Gomorrah in the Day of
Judgment than for that city. Inasmuch as Ye
have done it unto one of the least of these,
my brethren, Ye have done it unto me.

By the mid-1970s virtually all of the Children of God
colonies had left America. The group reappeared
briefly in the media when one of David Berg's own
daughters fled the cult and publicly accused her father
of incest. But that was the last I heard of them until the
arrests in Argentina in September 1993.

The New York Times article stated that the whereabouts of David Berg, now seventy-four, were still unknown. Twenty years earlier I had been told that Berg
did not appear in public because he was in very poor
health. He is clearly a man with a strong instinct for
self-preservation. His followers may suffer—the papers
reported that weeks later many were still in an Argentine jail. That could hardly be a pleasant experience,
but Berg himself would not share in the hardships. The
Times also reported that the Children of God had returned to Huntington Beach, California, where the cult
began. Are they planning a mass return to America,
which they had once so confidently predicted would
be destroyed? Only time will tell.

Could the charges of child abuse have been true?
I saw no evidence of child abuse in the group I visited,
though all of the children in that group were under
three years of age.

After the arrest, Children of God leaders issued a
statement denying all the charges and claiming that
they were the victims of religious persecution. The
Times article noted that after similar raids in Australia

and Spain, charges against the group were dropped for lack of evidence. Accusations of child abuse are now almost routine in connection with cults.

And yet—given what I knew about the Children of God philosophy and activities—I did not find the media accounts, sensational as they were, entirely incredible, or even surprising.

CULTS:
FEAR AND REALITY

A few final thoughts on the subject of cults are in order. There are hundreds of groups, perhaps even a few thousand, in the United States today that might be considered cults. Most are quite small and short-lived. And most are essentially harmless. We may disagree with, even despise, what many of these cults believe and the way they live. But one of the basic principles upon which this nation is built is that so long as people are doing no harm to others, they have a right to believe and live as they wish, no matter what the rest of us think of them.

It is impossible to make an accurate estimate of the number of people who are currently involved in cults, but compared to the total population of the country the percentage has to be quite small. Since cults have about them an aura of the mysterious and exotic, they get a great deal of attention from the media—far more than their numbers deserve—and that makes the average person think that they are much more numerous and much more powerful than they really are.

There are numerous organizations and individuals—from churches to law enforcement officials and psychologists—who depend for their fund-raising or their very existence on scaring people about what they perceive to be the danger from cults that threatens the youth of America. These people are not necessarily one bit more believable than those who speak *for* the cults. With the current hysteria over secret satanic cults, it may well be that innocent people are in greater danger from cult opponents than they are from cultists themselves.

Studies of cults indicate that the dropout rate is extremely high. Most people who join stay only a few weeks or months. Some may drift on to another group, still seeking an elusive answer. Most rejoin the mainstream of society, and are not permanently scarred or altered by the cult experience.

Cults possess no magical, mystical, psychological, or other kind of powers to control people's lives or thoughts. A cult can not pluck a perfectly normal, well-adjusted young person off the street, and in a matter of days turn him or her into a mindless zombie. People usually join a cult when they are at a crisis point in their lives, when they feel isolated or that their lives are without meaning or purpose.

While stories of kidnapping and brutal, forced conversion along the lines of the Patty Hearst case are extremely rare, the cults do apply heavy psychological pressure to keep their members within the group. But it is a pressure that can be, and usually is, resisted quite successfully. That's why the dropout and defection rate is so high.

In short, the cult menace to young people—to you—is not as great as you may have been led to believe.

But that doesn't mean that there is no danger at all. No one can recall what happened in Waco or Jonestown, or the sad history of the Children of God, and not realize that for some people cults can be dangerous, even deadly.

A cult can provide a sense of moral certainty, even moral superiority, that many people need. It can provide family and friends for those who feel that the family and friends they have are inadequate. And it can provide a feeling of power for those who feel powerless. It can give a sense of security to those who desperately require such assurance. However, to get the friends, the security, and the rest, an individual must deliver himself or herself to the control of the cult leader. The leader may be good, kind, and wise, or homicidally insane, or anything in between. For some, there is no way of telling until it is too late.

A lot of leaders, like Jim Jones, who started out with the best of intentions, wound up committing the worst of crimes. Being surrounded day in and day out by people who believe you are nearly divine, who constantly praise you and do your bidding, can produce strange aberrations. No one can tell the leader that he is wrong, and he can easily lose touch with reality. Those who have surrendered their own will to the leader may feel that they are in too deep to back out, no matter how destructive and crazy the leader may have become.

Is there any protection? Most people simply don't join cults; what looks like "the answer" to a few appears dangerously stupid to the majority. But under the right conditions, almost anyone can be tempted. Perhaps the best advice was given by a man who could have been one of the most powerful cult leaders of modern times.

In the last years of the nineteenth and early years of the twentieth century, there was a religious movement called Theosophy. Theosophy still exists today, but it is a very pale shadow of what it once was. Theosophy was the creation of Russian adventuress Helena Petrovina Blavatsky. It is a mixture of Eastern religions, specifically the Hindu religion, and Madame Blavatsky's own wild imaginings. Over the years Theosophy gained a large number of adherents throughout the world. It was most influential among the British in India and among some Indians.

Those who took over the Theosophical Society after Madame Blavatsky's death became convinced that a young Indian boy, Jiddu Krishnamurti, would become the new Messiah. The Theosophists spent years training the boy for his mission. He grew into a handsome man who simply radiated charismatic charm; when he appeared at meetings devout Theosophists would prostrate themselves before him. Krishnamurti, however, became increasingly uncomfortable with the adulation. He had doubts about his mission.

In 1929, Krishnamurti appeared before a gathering of thousands of the faithful, and informed them that he was no Messiah. He dissolved the organization that he was supposed to lead, and told the shocked crowd that people didn't need the kind of leader they wanted him to be, that no matter how difficult life is we should all try to find our own way. Quite simply, he said that we should think for ourselves.

A cult will hold no dangers for anyone who adopts that philosophy.

NOTES

CHAPTER ONE

By mid-October 1993, two government reports had been issued on the destruction of the Branch Davidian compound. The first severely criticized the initial raid by agents of the Bureau of Alcohol, Tobacco and Firearms. The second report covers the events from the time the standoff began to the fiery end of the compound. This report indicates that there were many suicides, and that the fire may have been started by cult members themselves. Criticism of the FBI and the Justice Department was minimal. This report has been widely denounced as a whitewash. In February 1994, almost exactly a year after the first disasterous raid on the Branch Davidian compound, a Texas jury acquitted eleven surviving members of the cult of murder charges connected with the killing of federal agents. Five were convicted of the less serious charge of manslaughter.

CHAPTER TWO

Though the Lubavitchers are a large, well-known group, which often courts publicity with full-page ads and billboards, the workings of the movement do not often receive coverage in the mainstream press. Most of the information on the movement in this chapter comes from *The Forward*, a weekly Jewish newspaper published in New York.

CHAPTER THREE

Nothing more clearly shows the almost supernatural attitude the public had adopted toward "brainwashing" than the 1962 John Frankenheimer film *The Manchurian Candidate*. Based on a novel by Richard Condon, it is available on videotape. Though it was clearly meant as a fantasy/thriller, it touched on people's real beliefs and fears.

CHAPTER FOUR

Though several books have been written on the Patty Hearst case, they all seem to have a particular ax to grind. The best way to get a feel of the impact of the kidnapping is to consult *The New York Times* summaries of the year's events for 1974 and 1975. The number of articles on this one case that appeared in what is generally considered the U.S. "paper of record" is quite remarkable.

The duPont/LaRouche case is covered in detail in the article "Blueblood War" in the April 1993 issue of *Vanity Fair*.

CHAPTER FIVE

The changing popular perception of the devil—and Satanism—can be traced through the following films, all of which are available on videotape: *The Devil and Daniel Webster* (originally released under the title *All That Money Can Buy*), 1941; *Damn Yankees*, 1958; *Rosemary's Baby*, 1968; and *The Exorcist*, 1973.

CHAPTER SIX

Two excellent articles on satanic cult claims appear in the Spring 1990 issue of *Skeptical Inquirer:* "Police Pursuit of Satanic Crime," by Robert D. Hicks, and "The Spread of Satanic-Cult Rumors," by Jeffrey S. Victor.

A detailed and truly frightening exposé of what can happen when a community is gripped by satanic cult fears can be found in a two-part article, "Remembering Satan," by Lawrence Wright, which appeared in the May 17 and May 24, 1993, issues of *The New Yorker.*

Robert Sheaffer's comments on Satanic cults appear in his "Psychic Vibrations" column in the Summer 1993 issue of *The Skeptical Inquirer.*

The murderous cultists in Matamoros, Mexico, seem to have been heavily influenced by the 1987 John Schlesinger film *The Believers.*

CHAPTER SEVEN

Even the popular 1970s sitcom *Bewitched* has come under attack from some religious fundamentalists. I have the impression that the series has not been rerun nearly as frequently as other, often less popular, sitcoms of that period.

CHAPTER EIGHT

The article that made TM scientifically respectable was "Physiological Effects of Transcendental Meditation," by Robert Keith Wallace. It appeared in the March 27, 1970, issue of *Science.*

CHAPTER NINE

Articles on the arrest of COG members in Argentina appeared in *The New York Times* on September 3 and 26, 1993.

BIBLIOGRAPHY

Ahlstrom, Sydney E. *A Religious History of the American People*. New Haven: Yale University Press, 1972.

Bach, Marcus. *Strange Sects and Curious Cults*. New York: Dodd Mead, 1961

Buckland, Raymond. *Witchcraft from the Inside*. St. Paul: Llewellyn Publications, 1971.

Cohen, Daniel. *The New Believers: Young Religion in America*. New York: Evans, 1975.

Cohn, Norman. *Europe's Inner Demons*. New York: Basic Books, 1975.

————. *The Pursuit of the Millennium*. Fairlawn, NJ: Essential Books, 1959.

Crowley, Aleister. *The Book of Law* (reprint). York Beach, ME.: Samuel Weiser, 1976.

Eberle, Paul, and Shirley Eberle. *The Abuse of Innocence: The McMartin Preschool Trial*. Buffalo, NY: Prometheus Books, 1993.

Editors of Time-Life Books. *Manias and Delusions*. New York: Time-Life Books, 1992.

Gardner, Gerald. *Witchcraft Today*. London: Jerrolds, 1968.

Hall, Angus. *Strange Cults*. Garden City, NY: Doubleday, 1976.

Huysmans, J.K. *La-Bas (Down There)*. New York: Dover, 1972.

Kahaner, L. *Cults That Kill*. New York: Warner Books, 1988.

Kilduff, Marshall, and Ron Javers. *The Suicide Cult*. New York: Bantam, 1978.

LaVey, Anton S. *The Satanic Bible*. New York: Avon, 1969.

Lyons, Arthur. *Satan Wants You: The Cult of Devil Worshipers*. New York: The Mysterious Press, 1988.

Masters, Anthony. *The Devil's Dominion*. New York: Putnam, 1978.

MacKenzie, Norman (editor). *Secret Societies*. New York: Holt, Rinehart and Winston. 1967.

Melton, J. Gordon. *Encyclopedic Handbook of Cults in America*. New York: Garland, 1986.

Moody, Jess. *The Jesus Freaks*. Waco, TX: Word Books, 1973.

Needleman, Jacob. *The New Religions*. New York: Doubleday, 1970.

Noyes, John Humphrey. *Strange Cults and Utopias of 19th Century America* (reprint). New York: Dover, 1966.

Reiterman, Tim, and John Jacobs. *Raven: The Untold Story of the Rev. Jim Jones and His People*. New York: Dutton, 1982.

Rhodes, H.T.E. *The Satanic Mass*. London: Rider, 1954.

Smith, Michelle, and Lawrence Pazder. *Michelle Remembers*. New York: Congdon and Lattes, 1980.

Snook, John B. *Going Further: Life and Death Religion in America*. Englewood Cliffs, NJ: Prentice-Hall, 1973.

Steiger, Brad, and Warren Smith. *Satan's Assassins*. New York: Lancer Books, 1971.

Victor, Jeffrey S. *Satanic Panic: The Creation of a Contemporary Legend*. Peru, IL: Open Court Publishing, 1993.

Waite, Arthur Edward. *The Book of Ceremonial Magic* (reprint). New York: Bell Publishing, 1959.

Waugh, Charles, and Martin Greenberg (editors). *Cults! An Anthology of Secret Societies, Sects and the Supernatural*. New York: Beaufort Books, 1983.

INDEX

Ingram, Paul, 87, 88
Inspirationists, 21
Israel, 28

Jesus Movement, 49–52
Jesus People (Jesus Freaks), 121
Joan of Arc, 93
Jones, Jim, 14–17, 19, 32, 74, 134
Jones, Larry, 89
Jonestown Tragedy, 14, *18*, 19
Judaism, 26, 59

Kahaner, Larry, 82–83
Kelly, Galen, 56, 57
Kohoutek, 122–123
Korean War, 41–44
Koresh, David, 7, 8, *9*, 10–13, 32, 74, 111
Koreshanity, 111–112
Krishnamurti, Jiddu, 135

La-Bas (Down There) (Huysmans), 63, *64*
Lanning, Kenneth V., 86
LaRouche, Lyndon, 53–54, *55*, 56
LaVey, Anton Szandor, 67–68, *69*, 70–71, 74, 86, 101
Levin, Ira, 65
Listen, Little Man! (Reich), 30
Lubavitchers, 26, *27*, 28–29

Maharishi Mahesh Yogi, 108, *109*, 110, 111
Manchurian Candidate, The (Condon), 42, 49
Manichaeism, 59, 61

Mansfield, Jayne, 67
Manson, Charles, 71
Mantras, 110
Matamoros, Mexico, 86
Medical cults, 29–31
Michelle Remembers (Smith and Pazder), 79, 80
Mind control, 33, 34–44
Moon, Sun Myung, 113, *114*, 115–116
Moravians, 21
Mormon Church, 22–23, *24*, 25
Muammar al-Qaddafi, 123
Murray, Margaret, 93, 94

Neo-Paganism, 98
New Age Religion, 58, 101
Newton, Saul, 106, 107
Nuclear war, 14–15
Nude rites, 95–96

Ofshe, Richard, 88
Old Religion, 94, 95, 97, 98
Orgone energy, 30–31

PACT (People Against Cult Therapy), 107
Park, Chung Hee, 115
Patrick, Ted, 50–52
Paul VI, Pope, 77
Pavlov, Ivan, 39, 41
Pazder, Lawrence, 79
Peoples Temple, 14–17, *18*, 19, 20, 32
Polygamy, 25, 126
Possession, 34, 76–77
Prisoners of war (POWs), 41–44

143